RYERSON OF UPPER CANADA

RYERSON OF UPPER CANADA

Clara Thomas

THE RYERSON PRESS TORONTO

© CLARA THOMAS, 1969

Published 1969

SBN 7700 0268 4

Library of Congress Catalog Card Number: 70-84983

PRINTED AND BOUND IN CANADA BY THE RYERSON PRESS, TORONTO

To my grandparents

SAMUEL AND MARTHA McCANDLESS
WILLIAM AND RACHEL SULLIVAN

> *. . . we are land-*
> *plowers   nightskaters*
> *we are seafarers in the*
> *flood who journey out*
> *in the barnboat to touch*
> *the broken leaf   to hear*
> *the dove   to brush through*
> *the boundaries of what-*
> *ever keeps us from being*
> *the wide new world*

"THE EIGHT-SIDED WHITE BARN"
by Miriam Waddington

Preface

Ryerson of Upper Canada is an attempt at the portrayal of a man and his times, of the circumstances which moulded him, and of his work and his achievement as a nineteenth-century educator. He lived and preached among the people of Upper Canada in the early days of its development; because he knew the people, he was particularly fitted to set in effective motion and, for thirty years to administer, the public school system of the province.

In many ways Egerton Ryerson can be seen as a representative Upper Canadian of the nineteenth century, embodying both the strengths and the limitations of a host of men whose talents and whose opportunities were fewer. Ryerson, the individual, has been effectively obscured by the triple-faced mask of Methodist-Journalist-Educator which he wore for the world and through which posterity viewed him. Only the massive and definitive works of Professor Sissons began to unmask both the man and his times; for them I am grateful, as any future biographer of Ryerson must always be.

I am also grateful for much interest and assistance during the making of this book: to Libraries and their Librarians—the Reverend John Bowmer and Miss Joan Gilbert, of the Wesley Archives in London, England; Mrs. Joan Wynn, of Lincoln College, Oxford; Miss Lorna Fraser, of Victoria University, University of Toronto, and Professor J. J. Talman and Miss Lilian Benson, of the University of Western Ontario, in London.

To Dr. Paul Fleck and my friends and colleagues of the English Department, U.W.O., who provided me with working facilities and congeniality during my writing of the book; to the invaluable research and manuscript assistance of Mrs. Marja Moens and the careful editing of Mr. Frank Flemington of The Ryerson Press; to the historical sense and the cooperation of my husband, Morley Thomas, and our sons Stephen and John; the encouragement of Dr. Francess Halpenny; the permission of Victoria University to quote from the manuscripts in their Ryerson collection, of Clarke Irwin, publishers, to quote material from Sissons' *Egerton Ryerson*, of Mrs. Miriam Waddington to use her poem, "The Eight-Sided White Barn"; the provision of a Sabbatical leave by York University and of a Special Award by the Canada Council; to all of these agents of the book's completion, my thanks.

And finally, I am especially indebted to Professor Robin S. Harris, Innis College, University of Toronto, for his initial and continued encouragement and enthusiasm for this project. His permission to quote from the Harris letters, collected in *My Dearest Sophie*, has been very valuable to me, and his own works on education in this province and on Ryerson have been important source materials for this book.

CLARA THOMAS,
York University,
March, 1969.

Contents

Illustrations

To understand the epic victories of Shaftesbury, "the British Abraham Lincoln,' or of Barnardo, "the Emancipator of the Outcast Child," aside from the permeating influence of the Evangelical Revivals which inspired and nurtured their characters and crusades, is utterly impossible.

Exactly the same is true of the character and achievements of Wilberforce, Howard . . . Ryerson, Lincoln, Harriet Beecher Stowe, Florence Nightingale . . .

Bready, J. Wesley. *England: Before and After Wesley*. London, 1938.

Chapter 1

To Be a Ryerson

On his twenty-second birthday, March 24, 1825, Egerton Ryerson began his circuit-riding mission for the Methodist Connexion in Upper Canada. His addition to the teams of indefatigable saddle-bag preachers who carried the message of Christ within the organization and the Discipline of John Wesley, was certainly considered a distinct asset by the Connexion. John Carroll, its liveliest historian, speaks of the new recruit with great satisfaction, remembering hearing in boyhood "that another and a *third* son of old Col. R. had embraced religion, and had become a Methodist preacher. It was our good fortune to see and hear him after that. It was at a camp-meeting. We remember his text, 'O, Israel, thou hast destroyed thyself, but in me is thine help.' "[1]

Preaching his first sermons in a log schoolhouse at Saltfleet near Hamilton, in the light of a tallow candle pinned to the wall by a hunting knife, Ryerson was very far from having any confidence in himself as an agent of God's help to the Upper Canada Israel. Doubts about his own state of grace and about his ability to preach effectively made him sick with nerves. "So bowed down with temptation today, I almost resolved to return to my native place," he wrote, and to his Mother, "Let me know the state of your mind, and your opinion about my returning home." He never did become one of Canadian Methodism's most renowned pulpit orators as did his brother William, but he quickly gained confidence in his competence to preach and in the sincerity of his own beliefs. In two weeks the painful initiation was over: "I feel encouraged to continue on."[2]

His commitment to Methodist preaching had been taken against his father's strong disapproval and at the cost of his more worldly ambitions towards the study of law. Furthermore, someone in the

1

Church of England had instituted some negotiation for his services as a preacher. This position with all its "advantageous attractions with regard to this world,"[3] he could have accepted with confidence, assured of his father's pride in him and of his own temperamental easiness within the decorum of the Establishment, for he was conservative by nature. He would also have been secure within the traditional, cultural precedent of Anglicanism for the lifelong, impassioned, personal pursuit of learning on which he was already well embarked. But his choice, though difficult, was to him clearly God-directed: "My heart is united with the Methodists, my soul is one with theirs; my labours are acceptable, and they are anxious that I should continue with them. I believe in their Articles, I approve of their Constitution, and I believe them to be of the Church of Christ."[4] The Methodists were, indeed, anxious enough to engage his services in their Ministry that they provided him with a horse and saddle. He began his journeying as a temporary replacement on the Niagara Circuit for his brother William who was temporarily worn out and dangerously ill.

The young Ryerson was, by the standards of his contemporaries, a fine, dignified and fitting figure of a preacher. John Carroll, obviously influenced by the nineteenth century's delight in amateur phrenology as well as by its preference for a man who looked well-fed, describes him as "fat and boyish-looking, like Spurgeon, only with a far more intellectual-looking face." His "crayon," as Carroll called his sketch, continues his enthusiasm:

The physique and physiognomy of our hero, whether in youth or riper years, has been such as became our notions of a great man. Rather over than under the medium size—well proportioned—fair complexioned—with large, speaking blue eyes—large nose, more Jewish than either Grecian or Roman—and then such a head! large, full, well-balanced, without any sharp prominences, but gently embossed all over like a shield. The mass of brain before the ears is greater in him than any man we wot of. The height, and breadth, and fulness of that forehead is remarked by all observers.[5]

Certainly if the portrait, painted in England by Andrew Gush when Ryerson was in his early thirties, can be trusted as in any way a likeness, he was a handsome young man. He is dark, with wavy hair cut rather short for his day, well-assembled features and a strong straight nose. The pleasant, rather sweet beginning of a smile round his mouth is startlingly contradicted and enhanced by a searching, melancholy intensity of gaze from large and heavy-lidded eyes. In this early portrait he is, in fact, a romantic looking young man who wears his side-burns, his white stock and broad coat-collar with an air that suggests far more elegance of mind and manner than North American Methodist preachers were accustomed to assume.[6]

The Ryersons were the kind of Upper Canadian family whose history and quality alone would be enough to make Methodists rejoice at the joining of their sons to the Connexion. Neither they, nor any who knew them, ever forgot that they had come to Norfolk County, on Lake Erie, as United Empire Loyalists;[7] the father, Joseph, and three of his sons had served as patriot militia men in the war of 1812; most important of all, visible evidence compared to the relatively tenuous honours of the spirit, they were sober, thrifty, prudent leaders of the community—on the squire level, in a day and among a people by no means unconscious or unappreciative of the values of a benevolent British-oriented social hierarchy. The Ryerson sons' becoming Methodist preachers had a very certain social symbolism, potentially powerful and, from the point of view of Methodists at least, beneficent to the entire population in its example.

Two Dutch Huguenot brothers, Martin and Adrian Reyerzoon, had come to New Amsterdam in 1647.[8] Their name was successively spelled Reyerz, Reyerse and finally it was anglicized to Ryerson about 1700. The Canadian branch of the family descended from brother Martin, whose grandson owned a fifty-acre farm running from what is today Broadway down to Wall Street. In 1711, he exchanged it for six hundred acres of wild land in New Jersey, at Pompton Plains, near Paterson, a good trade at the time. Egerton's father, Joseph, was born there in 1760, one of a family who split in their sympathies and allegiances during the Revolutionary War. One brother joined the Continental Army while one continued to live on the homestead and remained neutral, or tried to. Both the contending armies tramped through his farmland as on a thorough-fare, since it happened to lie on their lines of march. As they went, they raided. Three brothers—Francis, Samuel and Joseph—were loyal to Britain and in 1783 the latter two at least found it necessary, along with thousands of other Loyalists, to remove themselves to a climate congenial in spirit to their sympathies, though physically and economically anything but congenial.

Samuel was nine years older than Joseph; he had volunteered at the very beginning of the war, had been commissioned a Captain in the New Jersey volunteers upon his successful recruitment of sixty men and had served for the war's duration. His commission was granted to Samuel "Ryerse", either according to the old spelling or simply in mistake. That name he and his family retained, thereby adding a slight dimension both of variety and of confusion to the Ryerson-Ryerse chapter in Upper Canada's history. Joseph, only a boy at the war's outbreak, had rushed off to join the army too; around his military career there clings a faint, glamorous aura of derring-do. He was too slight to handle a heavy musket and so he was given a shot gun; he volunteered for the group going south to besiege Charleston and out-talked objections to his youth and inexperience; he became a notoriously daring and successful runner of despatches; and he was rewarded by a Lieutenancy in the New Jersey Volunteers.

Both Samuel and Joseph emigrated to New Brunswick in 1783, accepting the British offer of free transportation and a grant of land.[9] Both of them married in New Brunswick—Samuel's first wife died and his second was a girl from New York whose family were also Loyalist emigrés. Joseph married Mehetabel Stickney whose family had moved earlier to New Brunswick from New England, probably because of their British sympathies and certainly before the main Loyalist migration occurred. Like thousands of others, the brothers were refugees, exiles and losers, a hard experience for all and a tragic one for many. But for Joseph Ryerson there was bound to be more sense of hope and less of injury than for his older brother. A boy of fifteen at the war's outbreak, a young son among several older brothers, he would be aware of a lost security, but he had not had time to establish his own stake in the family land or to anticipate his own property.

Samuel was already a farmer when war broke out; when it ended he was over thirty. He had lost more than Joseph, including seven years of the peak physical strength especially precious to a farmer and essential for a pioneer. New Brunswick was disappointing, his land according to family legend was "sterile and uncongenial in soil and climate" and all his experience of it answered a contemporary description whose gloom bears an overpowering resemblance to the old Norsemen's notion of hell:

It [New Brunswick] has a winter of almost insufferable length and coldness . . . there are but a few inconsiderable spots fit to cultivate, and the land is covered with a cold spongy moss in place of grass. . . . Winter continues at least seven months in the year; the country is wrapt in the gloom of a perpetual fog; the mountains run down to the sea coast, and leave but here and there a spot to inhabit.[10]

Marriage compounded responsibilities, especially since his wife looked back towards the States with longing. Finally, in 1794, he packed up his family and returned to New York, settling temporarily on Long Island in the Brooklyn area. Again he suffered a large loss in time and his years of energy. He had hoped to stay in New York, but he found that an uncomfortable degree of prejudice was still operative against Loyalists and that it was still too soon to go back. His wife had certainly dreamed of staying, but personal tragedy played its large part in forcing a different decision upon her. She had borne eight children; three of them had died in New Brunswick and four more, seemingly healthy upon their arrival in New York, died with appalling suddenness, all within eight weeks— and there was only one little boy left. In such family desperation, it was not as hard as it would have seemed earlier to contemplate another trek into Canada. This time, Samuel decided to explore the possibilities of Upper Canada where he had reason to hope for some sign of favour from Governor Simcoe to whom he was known, both as Loyalist and good soldier.

Before the close of the war, Upper Canada had a reputation about as gloom-ridden as New Brunswick's: "[It was] known only as a region of dense wilderness and swamps, of venomous reptiles and beasts of prey, the hunting grounds and encampments of numerous Indian tribes, intense cold of winter, and with no other redeeming feature except abundance of game and fish."[11] By 1794, however, some thousands of Loyalists had been settled there and while still far from qualifying as one of the "sunny parts of America," it was soberly considered that this vast acreage was capable of supporting a numerous population and that it "afforded a sure and certain mode of safety and of honourable retreat."[12]

Mrs. Ryerse and the one remaining small son stayed in New York while Samuel and a friend set off to find the Niagara district and, hopefully, their promised land. For a forty-year-old such a journey was no glamorous adventure. Before leaving, Samuel paid due token to its difficulties and dangers by making his will, by formal farewells and by leaving instructions for the burial of his body on British soil only, should he die while travelling through the States. At journey's end, Simcoe did encourage his emigration, offering him 3000 acres, a captain's allowance according to the official grants policy, another 1200 as a settler, 1200 to his wife and each of his sons and 600 acres to each daughter.[13] Land was the cheapest commodity the British government had to give; practical help in settling was far harder to come by. Although immediately after the war the Government had committed itself to food subsidies, by 1794 the obligation to such a responsibility was officially past.

Samuel Ryerse made the return journey to New York, still unsure of his eventual place of settlement, but determined to try Upper Canada and to begin to move his family there as early in the spring as the route became passable. "It would be much easier for a family to go from Canada to China now, than it was to come from New York to Canada then," his daughter wrote in 1861. True enough—the sheer hard slogging required, daunting enough for strong men, was compounded to the edge of feasibility by the presence of women, children and household goods. But the acres of land were a shining target; Samuel had seen for himself the promise of benign abundance in the Niagara peninsula. And at his back was certainly the propelling awareness of years gone and of lost children, of bridges burned, both in New Brunswick and New York, and of this, the final choice that had to succeed. He was not at all the nomadic adventurer, challenged out of reason and caution by an undeveloped frontier; he was in spirit an exile, looking for a homeland recognizable to his needs and his memories. In every way he was impelled to find and settle a property for himself and his family on which and through which he and they could establish and hold a position that would satisfy their needs—and their needs certainly had to do with dignity as well as with survival.

As soon as the navigation season opened, Samuel, his wife, their one remaining child, George, one fifteen-year-old son of his first marriage, and some men he had hired as labourers, set out from New York, with a Captain Banta and his family, on a sloop packed with supplies and all the family goods they could bring. When they reached Albany, then one of the outposts of civilization, "a small Dutch town filled with Dutch people, Dutch comforts and frugality and Dutch cabbage," they went overland to Schenectady where they transferred their gear to a flat-bottomed "Durham" or "Schenectady boat" and then, with poles and oars, fought their way against the Mohawk river's strong current to the Oswego. To reach this stream they had to portage some two miles, and then follow it to Oswego on Lake Ontario; then they went as far as Queenston. At Niagara, Samuel saw Governor Simcoe, who advised him to settle in Norfolk County, which had recently been surveyed. The party lost no time in setting off again, anxious to find their spot, to draw their land and to have a shelter built before the cold came. Their bateau was portaged some nine to twelve miles around the Falls to Chippawa, they restocked their supplies, set out on Lake Erie and watched for the landmark formed by Long Point which had been described to them. The last hundred miles took them twelve days, the total journey probably about ten weeks:

When my father came within the bay formed by Long Point, he watched the coast for a favourable impression, and, after a scrutiny of many miles, the boat was run into a small creek, the high banks sloping gradually on each side.

Directions were given to the men to erect the tent for my mother. My father had not long been on shore before he decided that that should be his home. In wandering about, he came to an eminence which would, when the trees were felled, command a view of the harbour. He gazed around him for a few moments and said, "Here I will be buried."[14]

No Odyssey ends with the homeland reached. For a settler, the work of establishment occupied his own lifetime at least and, usually, that of his sons.

Four years later, Joseph and Mehetabel Ryerson, with six, perhaps seven children, arrived in Charlotteville, Norfolk County, from New Brunswick, to take up land near Samuel's and to refound their family fortunes in Upper Canada. Joseph, so much the younger, when every year's main asset for a farmer-settler was its total of his own physical strength to tame the forest, had not found the New Brunswick experience a failure. It is likely that he simply moved towards better chances and better land, influenced both by a certain satisfaction and optimism in the infrequent news he heard of Samuel and by a strong kinship that pulled him as it had at age fifteen, when he argued himself past age-restrictions to join the regiment that his older brother joined. In a day when the health and survival of children was of appalling chanciness, Joseph and Mehetabel had been free of the helpless parental sorrow so common and so well-known to Samuel and his wife. They had, in all, a family of nine flourishing children—George, Samuel, William, John, Mary and Mehetabel, were born in New Brunswick; Egerton, Edwy and probably Elizabeth were born in Upper Canada. The eldest, George, was born in 1791 and the youngest, Edwy, in 1811.

Joseph had been made a Captain of Militia while they were in New Brunswick and so he qualified for the same acreage as Samuel. Whatever the total munificence of forest that he accepted, and Egerton reports it as "about 2500 acres," he settled on a six-hundred-acre farm about halfway between Vittoria and Port Ryerse. He and his family profited not only from his brother's industry in the entire district, but also from the simple passage of time in an area under settlement. Four years had made a great difference, when, from 1795 on, every day brought its changes, as more and more prospective settlers looked over the land and liked what they saw.

The Ryerse-Ryerson group were founding families of the district and its leaders in many important ways. They were proud of their right to the official designation of "United Empire Loyalists" but in these early years of settlement they were neither self-consciously nor defensively "Loyalists". Only the war of 1812 and their subsequent strong ties to Methodism stirred the necessity for assertion and insistence on their Britishness and only growing nationalism, decades later, generated and perpetuated a kind of Loyalist cult. They were practical, hard-working men of the eighteenth century, with pride and a sense of substance and tradition that impelled them towards a certain standard and style of living in a new country. They had definite ideas about the society and the civilization they wanted, no doubts at all that what they wanted they could, in time, achieve— and "time" to their minds and to their bodies was a concept at once more leisurely and more spacious than the time we know. They carried with them their patterns of order and gave them practical expression in the houses they built whenever they could push beyond the pioneer shelter stage. Joseph Ryerson took more than twenty years to achieve the house he wanted, but when he built it in 1819, the symmetrical American Georgian of its design established both a remembered and a continuing dignity and confidence.[15]

Most of all, these men were North American farmers with a tradition of successful life on this continent already behind them and with the accumulated experience of several generations to bring to bear on their new land. They were unlikely to be either unduly expectant of what the land would offer or of the ease with which they could harvest what it had to offer. With everything still to be cleared, their lands seemed very little different in soil or in climate from the parts of New Jersey and New York that they knew. In fact, the sandy soil of Norfolk County had no long-term fertility for the grain crops which they expected to be their staples; compared to the soil of the Niagara peninsula, which had drawn Samuel to Upper Canada, this was poor stuff indeed. But if the land played its discouraging part in turning Joseph's sons from farming to the

Methodist ministry, that irony, like its present fertility in tobacco, was far in the future.[16]

At the moment the great difference was that Samuel and Joseph had to start all over again, in terms of labour and amenities, two, maybe three generations back of where the Revolutionary war had found them. Though the prospect was as daunting as the one which had faced the original Reyerzoon emigrant, they had all the generations' accumulation of marrow-deep experience in dealing with it. In this respect, as North Americans, they were far better fitted to be settlers in Upper Canada than any other group for decades to come. Necessity brought about quick adaptation in the Scottish, the Irish and the English, but the born and bred North Americans were bound to be just a little faster off the mark, especially when experience was joined to healthy family pride and a determination to found a new family property, as it was with the Ryerse-Ryerson brothers.

Five of the six sons of Joseph and Mehetabel Ryerson became Methodist ministers—George, William, John, Egerton and Edwy. Only the second son, Samuel, remained a farmer and he died young, in 1830, only thirty-six years old. They left few intimate, trival daily records of their lives behind them, partly because to men of their time only their public lives were open to the public's scrutiny, and partly because they were ministers with a strict sense of what was fitting to their calling. When they reminisced, it was of the spiritual and not the worldly journey; when they wrote letters to one another, and this they certainly did, with all of their times' devotion to the pen, they wrote first of their ministerial adventures. Their concerns were broad, and by no means always spiritual, for they were pushed and pulled inexorably into politics. But they had very little time for, or opinion of, the small talk and chatty detail that can furnish the bare walls of a past time.

Only in the odd remark, in the very obvious and sometimes moving affection existing between one "Rev'd. and Dear Brother" to another, and in Egerton's letters to his daughter, Sophie, did they write with the candid warmth of persons, not public men They would not have considered their letters suitable for the public eye; in fact, Egerton Ryerson's *The Story of My Life* is, by our autobiographical standards, nothing of the sort, but rather, a circumspect and circumscribed, rigidly edited public image for the instruction of nineteenth-century readers. In its brief opening chapter, "Sketch of Early Life," he gives a bare biographical outline of his family and an equally closed and secret outline of his early life, firmly shutting the door on intimacy with: "I know not that I can add anything to the foregoing story of my early life that would be worth writing or reading."[17]

Samuel Ryerse's daughter, Amelia, made splendid compensation for the austerity of the records among her uncle's children. Born in 1798, after the family came to Upper Canada, Amelia became Mrs. Harris, wife of the able and energetic John Harris, a former Master of the Royal Navy, who settled in London and became very much a man of its affairs and of the district's. John and Amelia Harris built Eldon House, above the banks of the Thames; they, their home and later, their large family, became an early focal point of social stability and confidence during the raw, growing years of the London district.[18]

In the 1850's Amelia wrote down her memoirs of the early days with a simple clarity that seems her own voice talking. Her first cousin and friend, Egerton, printed them when late in life he wrote *The Loyalists of America and Their Times*. He did not share all of her memories for he was five years younger than she, and his father had settled near Woodhouse, a few miles inland from his brother Samuel at Port Ryerse. However, both Amelia[19] and Egerton were among the early native-born children of the Long Point Settlement; they were schoolmates in the first log schoolhouse in the district; they remembered the same idiosyncracies of people and of place and they shared a common family tradition, both in the past and in the pioneer present of their childhood.[20]

Prudent settlers like Samuel and Joseph brought with them a year's supply of flour, salt pork, tea and salt—also nails and glass, since these could not be had nearer than Niagara. First a man threw up a three-sided shanty to shelter himself and his family and then, if there were other men with him or near him, they could put up a log-house in about twelve days, "cut and lay up the logs and chink them, put on a bark roof, cut holes for the windows and doors and build a chimney of mud and sticks. Sawing boards by hand for floor and doors, making sash and shingles, is an after and longer process.[21]

This shelter was sturdy, barring fire, and after the journey and the shanty, it seemed palatial. The Ryerses were spacious builders—two cabins attached gave them a parlour, two bedrooms, a kitchen and a garret. Shortly they had a cow, tied to the kitchen door at night and "fed upon browse, which kept her fat and in good heart—the men making a point of felling a maple tree each morning for her special benefit."

For fresh meat, a man simply walked out in the woods with his gun and spear:

My father had a couple of deer-hounds, and he used to go to the woods for his deer as a farmer would go to his fold for a sheep. Wild turkey and partridge were bagged with very little skill or exertion [he once killed six turkeys at one shot], and when the creek and lake were not frozen he need scarcely leave his own door to shoot ducks; but the great sporting ground ... is at the head of Long Point Bay. I have known him, several years later, return from there with twenty wild geese and one hundred ducks, the result of a few days' shooting. Pigeons were so plentiful, so late as 1810 and 1812, that they could be knocked down with poles.

The urgent goal was to clear some land and to plant maize, potatoes and vegetables for next year's food supply; to clear more land and always more for the wheat crops to come, for the orchard to spring from the carefully carried apple and pear pips and the peach, cherry and plum stones. If a man could find some other men to hire and had, as the Ryerse-Ryersons had, a little money to pay them, he set up, in effect, an establishment nearly as self-contained as a manor of the Middle Ages.

Samuel's holding was like this: to get the lots he wanted he had agreed to build both a flour and a sawmill on them. From 1800 on, when the London district was organized, he was its Lieutenant-Colonel of Militia and Lieutenant of the county while Joseph was its High Sheriff. Before that Samuel had been the district's Justice of the Peace, settling all disputes as best he could—for the nearest Courts were held at Sandwich, nearly two hundred miles away—and responsible for all marrying and burying of the settlers, since the nearest Anglican clergyman who could officially perform these functions was at Niagara. Unofficially he was the settlement's doctor and dentist as well —"so popular did he become in that way, that in after years they used to entreat him to draw their teeth in preference to a medical man— The one did it gratuitously, the other, of course, charged."

These are mellow memories of hope and quick achievement, coloured by Amelia's maturity and by the conventions of the mid-nineteenth century, of successful crops and rural simplicity, when all the household sat in the evening netting the twine for fish-nets, hollowing out troughs for sugar-making, and the women and girls spun and wove flax into strong coarse linen for shirts and plaid for their own dresses. A courting couple like the hired girl, Jenny, and young Daniel McCall worked and chatted in the evening group and then,

It was customary on those occasions, when the family retired to bed, for the young man to get up and quietly put out the candles and cover the fire, if any; then take a seat by the side of his lady-love, and talk as others lovers do, I suppose, until twelve o'clock, when he would either take his leave and a walk of miles to his home that he might be early at work, or he would lie down for an hour or two with some of the boys and then be away before daylight.... Nor must you imagine that there was anything wrong in this system of wooing. It was the custom of the country in an early day....

During the lean year of 1797, when the grain crops failed, the hands ground out their own allotments of maize in the coffee-mill each evening. "They soon learned the exact quantity required, and each man ground his own allowance . . . the meal was made into johnny-cakes, eaten hot for breakfast, cold for dinner, and the remainder in mush with milk for supper; and upon this fare they enjoyed perfect good health, were always cheerful, and apparently happy."

The settlement grew quickly: in two or three years "in a half-circle of twenty miles, probably there was a population of a hundred. People had ceased to count the families on their fingers." Almost every day some traveller came to the door, often staying for a few days to lend a hand in any project then going forward. The only urgency of time was a natural one, having to do with the labour hours between light and darkness, the demands of the weather, the days of growing and harvesting, and with the progression of the seasons, and not with any arbitrary or exterior notion of how far or how fast a man should or could travel in a day. Consequently "during the summer season our house was never free from travellers; not that there was any particular merit due to our hospitality, for the man that would have closed his door against a traveller would have been looked upon as worse than a savage." It was a tiny, struggling, yet confident society with a charity which in retrospect seemed astonishing: "And yet crime was unknown in those days, as were locks and bolts. Theft was never heard of .... If a deer were killed, a piece was sent to each neighbour, and they, in turn, used to draw the seine, giving my father a share of the fish .... Education and station seemed to be lost sight of in the one general wish to be useful to each other, to make roads and improve the country...."

The picture of the past carries its full complement of darkness too. Pioneer economy never reached much more than subsistence level. "Few grew more than sufficient for their own consumption and that of the new-coming settler; but had they grown more, there was no market, and the price of wheat, until the war of 1812, was never more than half a dollar a bushel; maize, buckwheat, and rye, two shillings (York) a bushel." Some years the crops failed and the people balanced on the edge of famine; in the summer of 1796 only the Indians along the Grand River a little to the east had a maize crop, as only they had known how to preserve it from the raccoons, squirrels and bears, "which had invaded the settlements by thousands in search of food, as there were no nuts in the woods." The precious flocks of sheep were especially vulnerable, both to wolves and to their own silly helplessness:

But all their watching could not preserve them from the wolves. If they escaped by the greatest care for a year or two, and the flock increased to twenty or thirty, some unlucky day would find them reduced to ten or a dozen. A tree sometimes unobserved would fall across the fence, and the sheep would stray into the woods, which was fatal to them; or, the fastening to their pen would be left just one unlucky night not secured, and the morning would show a melancholy remainder of the fine flock that had been folded the night before. All of these mishaps were serious vexations....

Sometimes, often in fact, fire destroyed the log cabins with their precarious stick chimneys, but wooden dwellings were easily replaceable compared to the family treasures which they contained. "These things, linen, bedding, and some little articles of furniture, and various little knicknacks which were prized beyond their value—were a great loss; but the greatest loss was a box or two of books."

Darkest of all were the human losses—a lost child, when the Indians were rumoured to be habitual kidnappers, deaths in childbirth and from illness, especially the rampaging tuberculosis, and the settlement's first accidental death, by drowning:

They found his canoe drifted on shore, laden with game, vegetables and a few apples, his hat and an empty bottle of rum; but he was gone ... his wife used to wander along the lake shore, from early dawn until dark, with the hope that she might find his body. One day she saw a number of birds on a drift log that was half out of the water. By the side of this log lay the remains of her husband. The eagles had picked his eyes out, but had only commenced their feast.

Many of the settlers always carried with them the dream of going home again—and home was some American farmland, likely in New York State or New Jersey, softened by time and memory into warm, ample fertility and civilization. Almost none went back, however; they were held, first by necessity and then by choice, like Amelia's mother. Samuel Ryerse died of tuberculosis in 1812, sixty years old; just six days after his death war was declared. In the spring of 1814 an invading party of Americans landed unchallenged at Port Dover, because every able-bodied man in Norfolk county had been ordered to muster well inland at Brantford, after an American fleet of seven or eight ships had been sighted on Lake Erie.

On the 15th [May, 1814], as my mother and myself were sitting at breakfast, the dogs kept up an unusual barking. I went to the door to discover the cause; when I looked up, I saw the hill-side and fields, as far as the eye could reach, covered with American soldiers. They had marched from Port Dover to Ryerse. Two men stepped from the ranks, selected some large chips, and came into the room where we were standing, and took coals from the hearth without speaking a word. My mother knew instinctively what they were going to do. She went out and asked to see the commanding officer. A gentleman rode up to her and said he was the person she asked for. She entreated him to spare her property, and said she was a widow with a young family. He answered her civilly and respectfully, and expressed his regret that his orders were to burn, but that he would spare the house which he did; and he said, as a sort of justification for his burning, that the buildings were used as a barrack, and the mill furnished flour for British troops.

That invasion marked the end of a generation's work: "Very soon we saw columns of dark smoke arise from every building, and of what at early morn had been a prosperous homestead, at noon there remained only smouldering ruins." The war also marked for the Ryerses and for many others a real separation from America as "home." "It would not be easy to describe my mother's feelings as she looked at the desolation around her, and thought upon the past and the present; but there was no longer a wish to return to New York. My father's grave was there, and she looked to it as her resting-place."

The war brought some death and ruin and much bewildered resentment to the people; it forced on them the shadowy beginning of an Upper Canadian loyalty and identity that had not developed earlier because it had not, until invasion, seemed especially precious. The war also turned the government towards immigration policies restrictive to Americans and the official air became thick with suspicions about dire American influences, among these—as the Ryerson brothers were to know—Methodism and the work of the saddlebag preachers.

The church was in the forefront of the securities that the early settlers missed, its importance as a symbol of civilization and stability as great as its active spiritual functions. Mr. Addison of Niagara did not visit the Long Point Settlement until at least ten years after its founding—Amelia Ryerse, who was one of the many unbaptized children officially sanctified in the eyes of the church on that great day, was old enough to remember the event vividly: "Mr. Addison shook hands with every individual, and made some kind inquiry about their present or future welfare. The same God-hopeful smile passed over every face, and the same 'I thank you, sir, we find ourselves every year a little better off, and the country is improving.' 'If we only had a church and a clergyman we should have but little to complain of'."

However, the Baptists and the Methodists, though they did not officially qualify as clergymen, were at work in the settlement long before the Anglican church could begin to serve its people. The Woodhouse church near Vittoria, where Joseph and Mehetabel Ryerson are buried, already had a Methodist congregation in 1800. Amelia remained Anglican all her life with a polite skepticism towards the early Methodists' "open demonstration of feeling—the louder the more satisfactory" and their forcible, energetic sermons which, "if they had been printed *verbatim*, would have looked a sad jumble of words." But she gave full credit to their services among the people she knew so surely to be "God-hopeful." "Were they not the class of men who suited their hearers? They shared their poverty and entered into all their feelings; and although unlearned, they taught the one true doctrine—to serve God in spirit and in truth—and their lives bore testimony to their sincerity."

Chapter 2

To Be a Methodist

THE religious movement called Methodism—begun by John Wesley after his conversion in 1738 when, for the first time, he found what he had been seeking in Christianity and felt his heart "strangely warmed" —was ideally suited to conditions in a new land. Phenomenally successful in eighteenth-century England, it was adapted perfectly to a place where there was everything to do, where most people were poor, their greatest assets strength of will and strength of body, where life was hard and good fortune chancy, but where everything was to be gained if only the effort made were great enough. Its ministers were missionary clergy, its revival hymns sang of marching to glory and journeying to God, its growth was a spreading cell-growth pattern as effective and relentless as twitch-grass in a lawn. And above all, its very core was a dynamism of affirmation; doctrinally centred in free will, its believers triumphantly felt and proclaimed a power to act rather than to be acted upon that ordered their temporal as well as their spiritual lives.

Wesley had been born in 1703, the 15th—his brother Charles the 17th—in the family of Susanna and Samuel Wesley, rector of Epworth, in Lincolnshire. Samuel was a less effectual parental influence than Susanna; though his principles were strong and often well beyond strength to stubbornness, he had little real sympathy for the people of his parish and in financial matters he was so careless that at one time he was detained for a year in Lincoln castle, a prisoner for debt. Susanna was, however, a woman whose will and intelligence were so strong, so balanced, and so undeviatingly channelled into the paths of Protestant virtue that to read of her is to comprehend the enormous, enduring power of the Protestant matriarchal image. The imagination clothes her in the classic robes of a Ceres or a Minerva

16

more readily than in the blue innocence of a sorrowing Madonna. The proverbial "who can find a virtuous woman? for her price is far above rubies" is totally, affirmatively answered by Susanna Annesley Wesley's wife. Because her children remembered love and trust as well as the rigours of her educational system, she also won the proverbial award: her children did "arise and call her blessed."

Early in John Wesley's ministry, he recognized that educating the people was a very large part and necessity of his mission. Characteristically, he set out to fill the need himself, work by work and book by book adding to his almost incredibly voluminous writing: journals, sermons, correspondence, treatises on education and text-books. The unabashed confidence of "I look upon all the world as my parish" was supported by his total commitment to the design and purpose of his God: "Thou hast said 'If any be willing to do Thy will, he shall know.' I am willing to do, let me know Thy will . . . and what I thus learn, I teach." He remembered the remarkable success of his mother's teaching methods and he promoted both her attitudes and her methods in his writings. Susanna lived to a very old age, and long before her death she had become a legendary figure among Methodists, as long after her death she remained both practical pattern and symbol of their feminine ideal. She somehow combined successfully, daunting virtue, formidable pedagogy, suitable female humility, and benign love—the archetypal Woman-Teacher-Wife-Mother-Methodist:

Dear Son,   *July 24, 1732*

According to your desire, I have collected the principal rules I observed in educating my family; which I now send you as they occurred to my mind, and you may (if you think they can be of any use to any) dispose of them in what order you please.

The children were always put into a regular method of living, in such things as they were capable of, from their birth; as in dressing, undressing, changing their linen and so on. . . .

When turned a year old (and some before), they were taught to fear the rod and to cry softly; by which means they escaped abundance of correction they might otherwise have had; and that most odious noise of the crying of children was rarely heard in the house, but the family usually lived in as much quietness as if there had not been a child among them. . . .

In order to form the minds of children, the first thing to be done is to conquer their will and bring them to an obedient temper. . . . Whenever a child is corrected, it must be conquered; and this will be no hard matter to do if it be not grown headstrong by too much indulgence. And when the will of a child is totally subdued and it is brought to revere and stand in awe of the parents, then a great many childish follies and inadvertences may be passed by....

I insist upon conquering the will of children betimes, because this is the only strong and rational foundation of a religious education; without which both precept and example will be ineffectual. But when this is thoroughly done, then a child is capable of being governed by the reason and piety of its parents, till its own understanding comes to maturity and the principles of religion have taken root in the mind....

None of them were taught to read till five years old, except Kezzy, in whose case I was overruled; and she was more years learning than the rest had been months. The way of teaching was this: The day before a child began to learn, the house was set in order, everyone's work appointed them, and a charge given that none should come into the room from nine till twelve, or from two till five, which, you know, were our school hours. One day was allowed the child wherein to learn its letters; and each of them did in that time know all its letters, great and small, except Molly and Nancy, who were a day and a half before they knew them perfectly; for which I then thought them very dull; but since I observed how long many children are learning the hornbook, I have changed my opinion.

But the reason I thought them so then was because the rest learned so readily; and your brother Samuel, who was the first child I ever taught, learned the alphabet in a few hours. He was five years old on February 10; the next day he began to learn, and as soon as he knew the letters, began at the first chapter of Genesis. He was taught to spell the first verse, then to read it over and over, till he could read it offhand without any hesitation, so on to the second, and so on, till he took ten verses for a lesson, which he quickly did. Easter fell low that year, and by Whitsuntide he could read a chapter very well; for he read continually and had such a prodigious memory that I cannot remember ever to have told him the same word twice.[1]

Susanna Wesley's child-rearing principles and practices are always memorable for the sincerely meant and confident tone of their antiquarian rigours, but there is nothing in them radical to their time and its beliefs. Their prime importance lies in her total conviction as to their suitability and success, and in the acquiescence of her most influential son, beyond mere agreement to promotion in his own pedagogy, and so influential far beyond his time and place.

Both by religious conviction and in answer to the inescapable daylight realities of the eighteenth century, Susanna Wesley educated her children for their souls' immortality. Their bodies' mortality was all too evident as she watched thirteen of her nineteen children die in youth or very early maturity. The deaths were in no extraordinary numbers in her time and place; they were "the will of God," and not to be railed at by the virtuous who knew, all too well, that "whom the Lord loveth, he chasteneth." On the other hand, God's mercy was not to be missed or ignored, and the saving of John from a fire in the Rectory, when he was five, his mother always saw as a miracle of direct Divine intervention. He had been in fact "a brand snatch'd from the burning" and she knew that a great purpose was in God's plan for him.

It was this sense of mission and destiny, which John Wesley himself felt and accepted, that set him in the first level of movers of men. In any age he would have been a leader. He had all the qualifications: a tough, tireless, inquiring mind, enormous drive and tenacity of purpose, organizing ability, courage, both physical and intellectual, a hardy physique and painstaking attention to detail—"the infinite capacity for taking pains"—often quoted as the hallmark of genius. Above all he could see from the small cell to the large pattern, from today down a vista of years. He was a born administrator who, from the very first years of his itinerancy seemed to carry the entire blueprint for the development and consolidation of Methodism in his mind. He knew, not only where he was going, but where best to deploy his forces and he could be, and quite often was, both autocratic and expedient in the promotion of his plans.

He had graduated from Christ Church College, Oxford, and had become a clergyman of the Established Church and a Fellow of Lincoln College. His first strong impulse was a rejection of the superficiality of much of the eighteenth century's religious life in favour of a withdrawn and ascetic ideal. His own soul's salvation was to be achieved in a "Holy Society" with his brother and a few other earnest young men, by means of upright living, intense self-examination, and a rigorous "Discipline." He was both educated and humbled, however, by an unsuccessful missionary enterprise to Oglethorpe's recently-formed colony of Georgia. He was also strongly affected, both in personal faith and in a more brotherly-social ideal of the godly life, by the influence of Moravians who first impressed him with their depths of serenity during a storm on shipboard and whose community in Germany he later joined for some months.

The Methodist Revival of the eighteenth century was by no means the only movement towards the enlightenment of the great mass of England's poor and in protest against the Established Church's lethargy about reform and the active church-involvement of the people. It was, however, by far the strongest of all religious movements of the time, particularly as the century advanced and formerly rural people herded themselves into the industrializing towns whose mushroom-springing slums were beyond the power of any recognized establishment, Church or State, to adequately service. The revival was already well under-way, led by the renowned preacher, George Whitefield, when Wesley joined the field-preachers whose methods were at first rather offensive to him. "I could scarce reconcile myself to this strange way of preaching in the fields . . . having been all my life so tenacious of every point relating to decency and order, that I should have thought the saving of souls almost a sin, if it had not been done in a church. . . . At four in the afternoon, I submitted to be more vile and proclaimed in the highways the glad tidings of salvation."

Glad tidings, salvation, the love of God as an always active, moving, shaping power for change, always available to the seeking, repentant individual—these were the great dynamics of Methodism. Indefatigable itinerant preachers, huge open-air gatherings, sudden emotional conversions by the thousands, the rapid and vigorous spread to America, the singing, with Charles Wesley alone the writer of six thousand hymns—these are legendary in the history of Methodism, the visible evidence of its astonishing vigour. It is also necessary to remember that the continuing force of Methodism, the organization of the thousands into societies, within these into classes, the training of lay preachers for their care, the establishment of circuits of duty and the setting up of Conferences—all of this was achieved through the administrative skill of John Wesley. At no time did his plans include a break with the Established Church, with whom, he insisted, the Methodist Societies were "in connexion."

In 1784, Wesley was eighty-one years old. He had been organizing and preaching Methodism, with an estimated five thousand miles a year on horseback, for forty-six years. Methodists numbered about 100,000, and Wesley had distributed, for the consolidation of the Societies and the education of their members, donations of about £30,000, a huge amount in eighteenth-century purchasing power. He was an old man and he knew very well that after him there was little or no hope that authorities of the Church would move to preserve his work. He, therefore, took two steps which, while they ensured the continuance of the Societies at home and in America, made almost inevitable their break with the Anglican church. By legal "Deed of Declaration," he appointed a Conference of one hundred men and made that group his successor, thereby establishing in law a church body. For the Societies in America, from whom British-born missionaries had been ousted back to England during the war years, for whom there were no ordained clergy and about whom the Anglican bishopric seemed prepared to do exactly nothing, Wesley himself ordained two men (Richard Whatcoat and Thomas Vasey) as deacons. He followed this by consecrating as superintendent the Rev. Thomas Coke, who had been episcopally ordained, and by instructing him to ordain, on his return to America, Francis Asbury. Devout, determined, boundlessly energetic, adventuring Francis Asbury was a former English blacksmith, a gifted preacher, and American Methodism's renowned "prophet of the long road."[2]

"Ordination is separation," warned Charles Wesley, deploring his brother's action and predicting dire calamitous results. Separation was, indeed, accomplished in America by this one stroke and finally, in England, after bitter wrangling. But the effect in America, far from weakening the Methodist position, infused its missionary leaders with double purpose—still to save souls, to be sure, but now, also, to build the church that was swiftly taking shape as the Methodist Episcopal Church. Some of the steps taken in America by Coke and Asbury horrified John Wesley who either would not, or could not, see that they followed logically from his own handling of the ordination crisis, and from the sheer distance over which he could not stretch an effective paternal guiding hand.

Besides, the independent spirit of strong men in a young country combined with the powerful conviction of God's plan and God's power working through men, the essence of the Methodism that they all preached, gave Methodism in America an especially bouncing vitality. It was useless for Wesley to rebuke Coke and Asbury as he did for what seemed to him to be undue, dangerous ambition and over-weening pride: "How can you, how dare you suffer yourself to be called Bishop? I shudder, I start, at the very thought! Men may call me a knave or a fool, a rascal, a scoundrel and I am content; but they shall never by my consent call me Bishop! For my sake, for God's sake, for Christ's sake, put a full end to this!"

When Thomas Coke presided over the first American Methodist Conference in Baltimore, Francis Asbury refused to be superintendent simply in accordance with Wesley's nomination of him. He insisted that, before either he or Coke served office, they should be elected by a majority of their own ministry which then numbered eighty-one preachers. From that time the church moved with its own force, setting up its own structure to serve the needs of an ever-expanding and particularly a westward-expanding community.

He [Asbury] discovered soon after his arrival that the preachers were tending to concentrate their efforts on the towns that had a settled population. He saw quite clearly that to restrict the Methodist enterprise to these would remove it from the growing-points of American life, and he begged his seniors to keep the preachers travelling on the ever-extending frontiers. In the end he persuaded them to adopt a rule by which no preacher stayed anywhere for longer than six months—with the result that where the men of enterprise and initiative went, there went also the Methodist preacher as one of them, and the Methodist circuit-rider became one of the formative influences of American civilization. Asbury himself is said to have travelled more than a quarter of a million miles. . . .
For the fifty years from 1790 to 1840 the Methodist Episcopal Church increased with astonishing rapidity, powerfully led by the circuit-riders, who took the Methodist Gospel across the Alleghanies to the furthest reaches of the American advance. Their methods were crude, their message was stripped to the barest essentials. . . . But they succeeded. Asbury's objections to educational schemes were gradually overcome, and colleges and schools sprang up everywhere in the wake of the circuit-riders.[3]

This was the evangelical, and immensely effective missionary enterprise which attracted Egerton Ryerson and his brothers first as converts and then as preachers. The heart of its doctrine had been described and constantly repeated by Wesley; it was repeated by Egerton Ryerson as the foundation of Canadian Methodism: "I have again and again, with all the plainness I could, declared what our constant doctrines are; whereby we are distinguished only from heathens or nominal Christians; not from any that worship God in spirit and in truth. Our main doctrines, which include all the rest, are three—that of repentance, of faith, and of holiness. The first of these we account, as it were, the porch of religion; the next, the door; the third, religion itself.[4]

Poor, wretched men, sinners all, could not attain that third stage without being led, or driven, through the first two—the porch and the door. Methodist preachers, Wesley himself, who were convinced that conviction of one's sinfulness and repentance were the first necessary steps towards knowing God, preached to batter down their hearers' barriers, or the Devil's fortifications, against Divine Love. Detractors accused them of being dominated by cowardly fear and of operating in a spirit of servile bondage rather than of filial love.[5]

And in Canada, the first generation of Methodist preachers were called "the thundering legion"; for the thunder of their voices sounded throughout the backwoods settlements of Canada—"Repent and be converted."[6] The thunderings spoke with remarkable effectiveness of God's wrath, in pulpit oratory which often lacked the polished phrase, but never the powerful one; something of the hell-fire Puritan Calvinistic strain still resided in the more uninhibited of America's and Canada's preachers. "Smite them, O Lord, smite them," as a climax to a fiery oration had the power to pummel thousands into moral acquiescence and conformity at least. But there were also the many hearers who experienced the next stage—the conviction of inner change which was the goal of all of it and with change, the faith in a God whose love would transcend and transform the grim hard reality both of men's insufficiencies and of life's rigours.

The emphasis of Methodism upon ideals voiced a longing of humanity. It were not worth while much to sacrifice to attain a religion which burdened the soul with constant spiritual stress; but it was quite another thing to attain one, whose goal—visible and feasible—was perfect love. This ideal was brought within the range of the practical by a nice emphasis upon "the power, not ourselves, that works righteousness. . . ."[7]

William Losee was the first regular preacher-missionary sent into Canada in 1790 by Francis Asbury. He and the others who followed him had no official status. Even after 1798, when an Act was passed to extend the right to marry to other clergymen than those of the Church of England, the Methodists were, both by legal and social pressures, impeded and snubbed. But two unbeatable forces worked for them and their mission—they were unalterably convinced of the truth and power of the word they preached and of the way they organized their followers, and they were constantly vindicated and stimulated by the need and the gratitude of the people. Amelia Harris speaks for a host of "God-hopeful" pioneers who crucially needed both spiritual reassurance and the practical manifestations of the presence of a Church, symbolized in its minister, to give their lives the ritual ceremonies and patterns that are strong reassurances and bulwarks of social order.[8]

All this, then, was to be a Methodist in Upper Canada: to be, if you had the abilities and the means of learning, the direct inheritor of John Wesley's doctrinally based and closely argued evangelical "Connexion"; to accept, certainly, his "Discipline" for its pursuance, with certain adaptations that time and the breadth of the Atlantic had placed on it. Your conduct of a Christian life was not only the private concern of yourself and God, but, for your good and the church's it was regularly examined and pronounced as continuing in the faith or reprobated as wanting and no longer worthy. A "backslidden Methodist" was sternly warned; if incorrigible, at the next examination, he was expelled from the group of the faithful. A Minister submitted himself to an even sterner discipline; to begin with he resigned himself to poverty—a pittance in pay and the hospitality of settlers who were usually bed-rock poor themselves. His acceptance as a preacher depended on his public examination by the Conference members and his public performance before it. He was assigned a circuit by the Conference and he continued in it at their discretion, always subject to recall and change:

The itinerancy of the preachers, in the Methodist system, with some inconveniences, is on the whole rather to the advantage of the preachers, in giving a large field for the exercise of talent, and a greater number of people to profit, or for the pleasure of acquaintance and friendship, allowing also more room for observation and reflection— faculties most useful to the effectual preaching of the Gospel. The preachers are moved from one circuit to another every year, or two years; and the presiding elders change their districts every four years.[9]

The entire system was designed both for a proper training of the individual's humility and also for the continuance and growth of Methodism's own strength. Within a stable social order it was another microscopic society: when there was little or no social stability, Methodism often seemed to constitute the only order. In a new country its organization and its rules became shelter and bulwark to the people—this, as much as its message, was the source of its strength in Upper Canada.

The circuit-riders travelled constantly, stopping to preach in every settlement and gradually establishing a pattern of travel so that certain places became meeting centres and even certain times became as regular as weather and accidents of travel would allow. For food and for lodging they depended on the settlers. Like John Carroll, one of the best of them, who "plucked his sermons off the bushes as he rode along," they had no time and no place for leisure or scholarship. "In those days no 'home' was assigned the 'junior preacher' or indeed the senior either, if . . . he chanced to be *single*—they were expected to find a home 'wherever night overtook them'."[10] They got around huge circuits in travelling conditions that at best would be to us impossible, and at worst unimaginable. Carroll describes one part of the Belleville circuit:

The road from Salmon River to the Mission at that time, in spring and fall especially, I pronounce to have been the worst one to be called a road at all, that I ever travelled. The land was very low and level. It had once been causewayed; but it was decayed, and the logs were all afloat; so that it was at the jeopardy of a man's life that he undertook to ride through some parts of it. My method was to drive my horse before me, and jump from log to log. It was a country, too, . . . an excellent place for getting an appetite, but the worst for getting anything to eat. . . . An invitation to a feast, the last time I went down, consisting of damaged corn and rusty salt pork, in which the dogs had stuck their noses sundry times while the kettles stood on the hearth during divine service which preceded the dinner, was much the most formidable difficulty I had to dispose of the whole year.[11]

They had to be strong, confident men, physically and spiritually, the first Methodist preachers, and there is a kind of sunshine light-heartedness about their stories when John Carroll tells them. Preachers Case and Ryan, for instance, about 1805, in the ungodly town of Kingston, where "there was no society" and the "inhabitants were very irreligious," would ride into town, put their horses at an inn, lock arms and go singing down the street "Come let us march to Zion's hill".

By the time they had reached the market place, they usually had collected a large assembly. When together, Ryan usually preached, and Case exhorted, for which he had a peculiar gift. Ryan's stentorian voice resounded through the town, and was heard across the adjacent waters to the neighbouring points of land. They suffered no particular opposition, excepting a little annoyance from some of the baser sort, who sometimes tried to trip them off the butcher's block which constituted their rostrum; set fire to their hair, and then blow out their candle if it were in the night-season. This was accomplished one evening by a wicked sailor, who then sung out, "Come on, boys, and see the Devil dance on a butcher's block".[12]

By practised skill in dealing extemporaneously with their hecklers in even the roughest of crowds and by their indomitable, indestructible enthusiasm and sincerity, the preachers could almost always win for themselves an audience. As Carroll explains them, there were few scholars among them, but they were almost all "in advance of the great bulk of the people in intelligence. . . . When this consideration is joined to the fact of their religious knowledge and character, their conversation in the several families where they sojourned—and, be it remembered, they lived among the people—must have been of incalculable benefit to those families."[13]

They were also the first and the only booksellers among the rural people. They carried in their saddlebags cheap editions of the Bible, often the Lives and Sermons of Wesley and Coke, Murray's English Grammar and Morse's Geography, sometimes *Paradise Lost,* Young's *Night Thoughts* and Cowper's *Poems.* These were works considered not only as eminently suitable for the faithful, but as required reading for young men aspiring to be preachers, as were Goldsmith's histories of Rome, Greece and England, Wesley's *Natural Philosophy* and Prideaux and Shuckford's *Connections of the Old and New Testament.*[14] The Conference approved and encouraged the selling of books, partly as a function of the educational mission which was so firm a part of the Methodist tradition and partly out of their preachers' necessity; "for the little profits they made on books sold, went to supplement their very small allowances. Further, they had the use of the books themselves, both before and after they were sold. Thus their own and the people's improvement was promoted."[15]

They had their charlatans—the odd one who was more entertainer and peddler than preacher, like Samuel Coate, who "wore long hair, which flowed down on his shoulders, turning up in graceful curls. Every night, with his garters, he would tie up his beautiful locks, and every morning he would untie and comb them out, then allowing them repose on his shoulders and back."[16] He was so skilled a penman that he sometimes wrote the Lord's Prayer on his thumbnail. He was spoiled by easy popularity and turned out a bad lot altogether, leaving his wife and daughter in Canada, to have his handiwork, the Lord's Prayer written on a sixpence, engraved in England, and to sell copies of this wonder all over the British Isles at £2 each.

They also had their eccentrics, like Lorenzo Dow, so convinced of his vocation that he persisted in preaching even when told bluntly that his health, gifts, grace, learning and sobriety were not sufficient. When an American quarterly meeting dismissed him, "two or three handkerchiefs were soon wet through with tears; my heart was broke," said he, and he finally persuaded Francis Asbury to send him into Canada "to form a new circuit, and break up fresh ground. . . . A revival took place in those parts where I laboured, and the wilderness did bud and blossom as the rose. However, I was not the commander of my feelings. My mind was still drawn to the water; and Ireland was on my mind."[17] He left Canada for Ireland and left his strange legend, half noble, half pitiful, behind him: "Dow was not like other preachers, loving and practising rule and order, and resembling the orderly motions of the sun, moon and planets. He loved to do good, but his way of doing it was like the course of the comets, which come and go, and no one knows when they will come again. . . . No people ever complained that Lorenzo Dow remained too long in one place. His chief fault was, he did not remain long enough.[18]

But in general, the reputations of the Methodist preachers among the settlers range between a healthy camaraderie of good feeling and a real warmth of love and respect; between men like Darius Dunham, "scolding Dunham," who was even more effective than most in denouncing the "God-denying, God-forsaken, and hell-deserving" Sabbath-breakers and cheerfully aware of his reputation, to Irish Henry Ryan, whose "end was not so well as the beginning." He became the leader of a violent factional movement among the Methodists but in the early days all the people loved him. In an isolated community on the Plattsburgh circuit they were so grateful for his preaching and eager for his next visit that they "gathered, cut out the brush, felled and cut up some of the large trees in the way, and opened a tolerable path for his horse. Where the new path and the public road joined, they blazed a large tree, and wrote on it, with an index pointing to the new path, 'Brother Ryan, turn down here'."[19]

If, however, like Joseph Ryerson, you were a Tory, Anglican farmer, anxious to establish a place and a name in Upper Canada, you were not likely to welcome the Methodists' claiming your sons. Having emigrated once as a Loyalist, it was doubly hard to have any suspicion of American sympathies, however faint and stifled, attached to your family. Increasingly after the war of 1812, the Methodists *were* suspected and denounced in the violent, bitter press disputes of the day, accused of having American sympathies and of being under American influence. The reports were exaggerated, but, true enough, it was the American branch of Methodism that supplied the first wave of preachers to Upper Canada and American academies had trained those that were formally educated at all.

Then, too, the social stigma, slight at first, but growing as the population and the prejudice grew, was hard for an ambitious Anglican parent to bear. It ranged through all the gradations of snobbery, from coarse rejection of the preachers by those who were illiterate, unregenerate or uncaring, to brisk and pithy dismissal in the accents of solid Anglican, British-background country-folk—like Mrs. Poyser in George Eliot's *Adam Bede*, when she compared Mr. Irwine, the rector, with the Methodists:

It's summat-like to see such a man as that i' the desk of a Sunday. As I say to Poyser, it's like looking at a full crop of wheat, or a pasture with a fine dairy o' cows in it; it makes you think the world's comfortable-like. But as for such creatures as you Methodisses run after, I'd as soon go to look at a lot o' bare-ribbed runts on a common. Fine folks they are to tell you what's right, as look as if they'd never tasted nothing better than bacon-sword and sour-cake i' their lives.[20]

And most of the very few, comfortable few at the top of Upper Canada's embryonic social chain viewed the Methodists with some degree of distaste and alarm, suspecting them of a republican tinge and rejecting their crudities. For above all they asked for and expected a clergyman with a proper sense of what was due to each social degree in his charge. The saving of souls from a butcher's block in the Kingston market was altogether unseemly, certainly not to be condoned in their minuscule "society" where decorum was doubly precious because so frontier-fragile. They preferred, they *needed,* for their perilous security, to march as they believed the stars to march—"rank upon rank, the army of unalterable law"—they expected, in fact craved, clergymen whose conviction of the truth and fitness of Anglican doctrine was total and totally matched by a sense of the dignity and security of the Anglican Church Establishment.

The end of the American War, in 1814, was followed by one of those evangelical awakenings in Upper Canada, for which the Methodists were always preaching and praying—times when an epidemic of emotional fervour would sweep a district and seem to prove it under the direct and benign attention of God. George, William and John Ryerson—all of the New Brunswick-born family of Joseph and Mehetabel, and so considerably older than Egerton—were converted to Methodism, and perhaps their mother as well. Certainly from that time on she was openly a Methodist in her sympathies, and it may well be that her influence had worked in that direction from a much earlier day. However, Joseph was, in his son's words, "extremely opposed" to it—in fact, he bore with his three oldest sons' leaving property and agriculture for the economically rootless insecurity of an itinerant ministry only because he had no choice. They had been of fighting age when the war began, and they were certainly beyond his parental power to hold by the time it was over.

Egerton was a different matter. He was Joseph's hope for the farm and its future; he was strong, and a hard and clever worker. He was the son who was going to consolidate, build and prosper on what his father had painstakingly cleared and cropped. He worked well with his hands; when he was fourteen and his father finally built the long, porticoed white frame house that symbolized his family's success, its

past and its pride, Egerton worked with the carpenter for six months.
He was inspired by a life of Benjamin Franklin and its account "of his
mechanical education and of its uses to him in later years, during and
after the American Revolution, when he became Statesman, Ambas-
sador, and Philosopher. . . . During that time I learned to plane boards,
shingle and clapboard the house, make window frames and log
floors"[21] and to do the interior panelling on the dining-room walls, a
job which still gave him pride fifty years later.[22] In a new country
where physical strength and general handiness counted for real capital, it would have been hard to lose such a son to any profession. It was
almost unbearable to lose him to the Methodist ministry.

While the pervasive influence of his mother's and brothers' faith and
the excitement and soul-searching of the revival effected his conversion, Egerton did not, for several years, defy his father's authority
to formally join the Methodists, though he was committed to them
and attended meetings and services when he could. In particular he
credits his religious conversion with awakening him to the satisfaction
and challenge in learning that he never afterwards lost:

From that time I became a diligent student, and new quickness and
strength seemed to be imparted to my understanding and memory.
While working on the farm I did more than ordinary day's work, that
it might show how industrious instead of lazy, as some said, religion
made a person. I studied between three and six o'clock in the morning,
carried a book in my pocket during the day to improve odd moments
by reading or learning, and then reviewed my studies of the day aloud
while walking out in the evening.[23]

Whatever degree of rigour in child-training had been practised in
the Ryerson family, the will of Egerton had certainly not been broken
to parental authority. In fact, all of his life he worked best, felt
strongest and most justified when under fire. To command his own
total resources, he seemed to need to be strongly opposed, and he never,
from this time on, had the slightest difficulty in finding the required
battle situations. His father would have nothing to do with providing
him books or schooling as long as he went among the Methodists.
After all, in Joseph's opinion, education at Union College in Schenectady had done nothing for older brother George except to turn him
into a lazy preacher. This kind of opposition was simply a spur to
Egerton: "A kind friend offered to give me any book that I would
commit to memory, and submit to his examination of the same. In this
way I obtained my first Latin grammar, 'Watts on the Mind', and
'Watts Logic'."[24]

When, at eighteen, he was pressed to join the Methodists who had so far been allowing him the status of a member without his actual declaration, he decided to join them "in view of all possible consequences." Father and son then each played his part in total ritual stereotype: " 'Egerton, I understand you have joined the Methodists; you must either leave them or leave my house . . .' The next day I left home. . . ."[25]

To Joseph Ryerson, Methodism was socially unacceptable and, worse than that, unmanly; his revulsion was like a modern father's whose son has grown his hair long and joined the Flower People. It had been hard enough for a man who saw himself as a farmer-squire, of substance and influence in the district, to have to add to his comfortable picture three saddle-bag preachers in a church more fit for ridicule, in his opinion, than for reverence. Now, in Egerton's case, there was also, plainly and inescapably, the economic fact. He badly needed this son on the farm.

Egerton's will was at least as strong as his father's and his decision was inevitable, but he made his kind of amends. As soon as he had work himself, as a junior teacher in the London District Grammar School, he hired a labourer to take his place at home. "But although the farmer was the best hired man my Father had ever had, the result of his farm-productions during these two years did not equal those of the two years that I had been the chief labourer on the farm, and my Father came to me one day uttering the single sentence, 'Egerton, you must come home,' and then walked away."[26]

This is only the first record of the kind of sequence of events that was to occur often in Egerton Ryerson's life. Faced with choice, he often saw as he saw now, not one path to follow and one to reject, but two that might just both be navigated. In a day and among a people who saw choices in blacks and whites, one road to heaven and the other to hell, he developed balancing techniques of hair-raising success, a tight-rope agility that men viewed often with fury and deepest-dyed mistrust, and at best with alarm.

Now he went home and did the jobs his Father needed done: "I relinquished my engagement as teacher within a few days, engaging again on the farm with such determination and purpose that I ploughed every acre of ground for the season, cradled every stalk of wheat, rye, and oats, and mowed every spear of grass, pitched the whole, first on a waggon, and then from the waggon on the hay-mow or stack."[27] Furthermore, he continued hours of study as well, making "nearly, if not quite, as much progress in my studies as I had done while teaching school."[28] He was awesomely serious and obsessionally devoted to both learning and the Godly life, and his next venture, made after the harvest was in, not with his Father's approval, but certainly with a considerable mellowing of his attitudes, ended in complete breakdown.

Guided by his brother George, Egerton went to Hamilton to study under John Law at the Gore District Grammar School. Despite Law's concern and warnings about his health, he drove himself at "Classical Studies"—the endless preparation, translation and memorizing of Greek and Latin texts—with an intensity that ended after six months in breakdown and serious illness. "Brain fever" and "inflammation of the lungs," for which we read exhaustion and pneumonia, or near-pneumonia, nearly killed him. During its course he made one of the pacts with God so often entered upon in those days when His presence seemed close and personal and when His intervention could be expected to be dramatic and personal too: "I then and there vowed that if I should be restored to life and health, I would not follow my own counsels, but would yield to the openings and calls which might be made in the Church by its chief ministers. That very moment the cloud was removed; the light of the glory of God shone into my mind and heart with a splendour and power never before experienced. My Mother, entering the room a few moments after, exclaimed: 'Egerton, your countenance is changed, you are getting better!' "[29]

Joseph Ryerson lost, but with some grace, his bid to make his son a farmer-squire. He offered Egerton the deed to the farm if he would stay at home and work it, but they both knew it was useless: "One day, entering my room and seeing a manuscript lying on the bed, he asked me what I had been writing and wished me to read it. I had written a meditation on part of the last verse of the 73rd Psalm. . . . When I read to him what I had written my Father rose with a sigh, remarking: 'Egerton, I don't think you will ever return home again.' and he never afterwards mooted the subject, except in a general way."[30]

Chapter 3

An Ark of Exiles

Upper Canada in the 1820's and 1830's was an emergent province, with the tensions and pressures of rapid change, the necessity for quick assimilation of widely various groups and conditions of people, the compelling urgency to do everything at once—and fast—and the unrest and violent factionalism that the term implies in our time. During these decades, Ryerson travelled, preached and wrote. He learned to make a preacher's rhetoric, a talent for argument and a flair for journalism the tools of religion, and he found that all these were, in his time and place, inextricably bound up with politics. Most of all, he took his own measure, found his own powers and began to map and to clarify the areas of his future opportunities and responsibilities.

There was still the forest. Settlement spread back from the waterways as land was surveyed and opened by roads, but the country was vast and clearings were patchy. The forest still remained the primary element, to be navigated by the preachers, the peddlers and the travellers and to be beaten down into wheat fields and tame woodlots by the settlers. Each group saw the forest according to its own needs, desires and experiences; those who stayed to live, sometimes to prosper, had to win over it, against the fear of danger in its dark places and against its enormous, devouring energy of growth.

If your horse strayed away, and Ryerson's did, you were not only helpless to cover your circuit, but also you were bound to recall the most hateful way of impeding the Methodist preachers, practised by some brutalized scoffers—that of maiming their horses: " I have been considerably agitated in my mind. . . . The fatigue in searching for her has been considerable. Thank God she is found."[1] George Playter, as a young preacher could feel a pleasurable, romantic awe and fear in the midst of a storm in the forest: "A mighty wind came. The clouds jostled, one furiously struck the other. Lightning blazed. Thunder bellowed. Trees cracked and fell. Birds screeched. A wolf barked. Ruts became torrents; torrents became rivers. . . . The birds of the forest pierced the air with their wailings, and cried for the departure of the tempest."[2]

But Playter wrote from comfortable retrospect. Travellers in the forest in any weather heard the sound of a tree cracking and falling every fifteen minutes[3] and in a storm the immediacy of danger was only too evident: "In travelling today a tree fell across the road four or five rods before me, and another not far behind, but I escaped unhurt. . . . I felt that the Lord was indeed my protector. But whilst so narrowly escaping myself, two persons, a woman and her son, who were travelling a short distance behind me, were suddenly killed by the falling of a tree. . . ."[4]

Stories of starving, attacking wolves were current, more spine-chilling folk-lore than actual travellers' hazards, but the very possibility of their truth operated powerfully at first on the nerves of travellers. Emigrants were said to "generally keep glancing about from side to side of the road, expecting every minute to see a bear or a wolf dart out from every thicket they may pass."[5] In fact, wolves were sometimes a menace to sheep, but to travellers they were little more of a menace in the parts of Upper Canada then accessible than they are today; a travelling preacher could ride the roads and trails for fifteen years without seeing either.[6] But the horror of their legendary threat, sustained and elaborated in tale after tale, was caught and held in stories like this one:

He observed two long, lithe animals spring out of the woods towards his horse . . . great powerful animals with immense length of limb and depth of chest. . . . A shiver seemed to convulse her [the mare's] frame. . . . All the dread hunters' tales of lone trappers lost in the woods and their gnawed bones discovered in the spring beside their steel traps flashed through his mind like a thought of horror. . . . He now threw down his thick leather gauntlets with the hope of delaying them, but it only caused a detention of a few minutes while they greedily devoured them. . . . One of the brutes now made a spring for the mare's throat . . . the white foam fell from his mouth. . . . Lawrence could feel his hot breath on his naked hand. The fiendish glare of those eyes he never in all his life forgot. . . . If ever there was murder in a glance, it was in that of those demon-eyes. . . . One or other of them must die. . . .[7]

Many travellers and settlers progressed as Isaac Fidler, an Anglican minister, describes his progression, quite quickly from "unusual shudderings from the surrounding solitude and the uncertainty of my path," from feeling at first that these forests must "form impenetrable barriers to the settlers and are the confines of population," to confidence that any road or track would lead him into "cleared and open spots, before hidden from our sight, where sometimes one or two, and sometimes many families, are bosomed in the woods . . . till at last my mind became quite reconciled to wilderness scenes and derived a tranquil pleasure from their presence."[8] But there were also those, like Isaac Fidler's wife, who found life in the bush intolerable. She was one of the fortunate: the Fidlers could and did go home to England. Most settlers, once here, had no choice but to stay. Utter bed-rock necessity quite often bred strength and toughness of body and will—no one could either foresee or prevent the grey cold rockiness growing in the spirit and the imagination as well.

Among the things that men had made, there was, preeminently, British law. Its presence permeated the country and as men were restricted by it, so were they liberated, to live without fear of other men. It was not so much symbolized by imported red-coated troops, for these were few and stationed in scattered garrisons, or by courthouses, for there were few of these yet built, as embodied in a more homely and reassuring way in lawyers and Justices of the Peace, the law's functionaries.

There were rough little towns springing up at likely crossroads and mill sites, trading centres and the dispensers of the necessities of life and even some of its amenities. They were, in their own way and in their time, forts in the forest, not bristling with guns or red-coated troops, but supply bases and civilization-centres for the areas they served. In the oldest, the most secure and the most populated of them —in Kingston, Niagara-on-the-Lake, York and even in London— there were people already who had built and were building beyond subsistence-security to comfort and dignified, civilized standards of living and behaving. But by any cosmopolitan standards, even these were, at best, tight little towns where a very few people found some illusion of society and social security within rigid little walls of sect and class. Then there were no elegant Canadians, though a few of those who led and governed were expected to be elegant people and some others, like Mrs. Powell of York, aspired to be among them: "You know I am not addicted to extravagance in any personal indulgence, but in an aristocratical Government expenses must be incurred according to the station held; it would be improper for me to receive my company in a cotton gown to give them a joint of meat and a pudding, or to return their visit in a waggon."[9]

Some of the most vivid records of Upper Canada were written by those who were temporary travellers, adventurers and onlookers only, men like Sir George Head, an army officer whose responsibilities to Upper Canada were minimal and temporary and who looked upon the forests as a Heaven-ordained game preserve. In his own account of his travels from Halifax to Penetang, Head, like Robinson Crusoe, relates experiences with a rare calm and commonsense—and with Crusoe's tone of benign detachment from all other human beings:

I had directed my hut to be erected on the summit of the brow which rose close from the bay; and when I returned to the spot I found my servant busily arranging my different articles of property in an edifice which, if not equal in splendour to the renowned palace of Aladdin, had been, at least, completed nearly in as little time. By the help of a few poles and cedar boughs, I had now, such as it was, a house of my own. There were at least two sides with a back part, and the front was open; but a brilliant fire was blazing before it, big enough for the kitchen of the London Tavern, and in itself a world of comfort.[10]

There were a few adventuring women too, who, like Anna Jameson in the thirties, intrepidly went everywhere, to see everything and to tell all. Certainly Mrs. Jameson was fortified by a holiday patience for hardships and a security that derived from the comforting sense that here was not her own security. The land was a temporary challenge to her indomitable traveller's nature, and while abroad in the wilds she was buttressed by the consciousness of the consideration owing to her as "The Chancellor's Lady." Her interest in the people she met, unimpeded by social barriers, made her a unique reporter and commentator on the whole raw, rough and restless society, but she can write as she does, in tones which range from most sharply critical to most warmly sympathetic, only because the land is neither her essential home nor her permanent livelihood.

Henry Schoolcraft, American Indian agent at Michilimackinac, deeply rooted in North America both in his own life and in his Indian research interests, noted and speculated on a distortion of vision and perception among all the temporary travellers: "It seems to me that Englishmen and Englishwomen, for I have had a good many of both sexes to visit me recently, look on America very much as one does when he peeps through a magnifying glass on pictures of foreign scenes, and the picturesque ruins of old cities and the like. They are really very fine, but it is difficult to realize that such things are. It is all an optical deception."[11]

For those who came to stay, it was all a far, far different thing. The land beneath the forest trees was the golden chance for all. No matter what the difficulty of clearing and farming, the essential dream, security in a man's lifetime and a property to hand to his sons, was realizable. And it was at least as common for an ordinary man to acquire more land than he could possibly fence or farm as, in England, Ireland or Scotland, it was unlikely that he would ever have a deed of ownership to any at all. The optimism, the insistent hope have been sketched over and over again, sometimes with post-Confederation euphoria in simple-minded fiction like Joseph Hilts' *Among the Forest Trees,* which shows its true-blue manly hero, John Bushman, "a young man of about twenty-one or -two years of age, with his coat off and his sleeves rolled up, swinging an axe with as much dexterity as though he had been accustomed to that sort of work all his life: 'What are you doing here?' said one of the men ... 'Commencing life in the backwoods, ... I have no house, as yet, to invite you into, nor have I any chair to offer you. But both the house and the chair are on the list of things that I hope for in the not very distant future'."[12]

At about the same time and in the same mood, Isabella Valancy Crawford wrote of another John Bushman, heightened, romanticized and mythic in his sense of power, her Young Max of *Malcolm's Katie:*

> Swift fell the axe, swift follow'd roar on roar,
> Till the bare woodland bellow'd in its rage,
> As the first slain slow toppl'd to his fall.
> "O King of Desolation, art thou dead?"
> Thought Max, and laughing, heart and lips, leap't on
> The vast prone trunk. "And have I slain a King?
> Above his ashes will I build my house—
> No slave beneath its pillars, but—a King!"[13]

The emotions born of the realities of settlement were harder and grimmer than Max's, however; doggedness was required, bitterness often attended it: "The Canadian settler *hates* a tree, regards it as his natural enemy, as something to be destroyed, eradicated, annihilated by all and any means."[14] Why not? With perfect strength, good fortune and good weather a man could only clear an acre in three weeks and still the stumps remained, to be burned out, or to plough and plant around.

John Bushman's mate was, ideally, a type of the strong and godly woman whose perfect living pattern had been Susanna Wesley. In fact, however, it was usually only old age and endurance that could bring such strength and dignity. Upper Canadian emigrant women were commonly made drudges by work and childbearing, or lonely neurotics by their exile, and not until the next generation did their daughters begin to find, often to accept the dangerously powerful role which preachers, writers and journalists exhorted them to live—that of the Protestant "Mother", with all its sentimental trappings.

In the forefront of the past are those of more wealth, or more influence, or education, or competence than the others, those whose stories have been told: a Colonel Talbot, for instance, of aristocratic connections and military training, a rough, tough land-baron, but in his way an efficient colonist—also, finally, a lonely, crotchety, cantankerous, often bleary-eyed old man, who said, "Why yes, I'm very happy here"—and then sighed: "I have acomplished what I resolved to do—it is done. But I would not, if anyone was to offer me the universe, go through again the *horrors* I have undergone in farming this settlement."[15]

A Dunlop, a Gourlay, a MacNab, a Mackenzie, a John Strachan: these were men with strong, dynamic natures, large capacities for action, possessing dreams and sometimes possessed by them. A MacGrath of Erindale, a Vansittart of Woodstock, a Langton, a Strickland, a Traill of Peterborough, a Moodie of Belleville, these are quieter, humbler, more modest people. Their stories have less colour and glamour and they move, not from height to depth, but within a middle range of reasonable expectation and temperate achievement. These are the people who knew best and never lost sight of what they had come for; the records they left and that others left of them tell of discouragements and many reverses. But they also tell preeminently of people who insistently believed that they would achieve what they had come for—property to develop and pass on and an embryonic society in which they could live and move without too radical a departure from British-oriented preferences and expectations. This confidence, backed by lifetimes of effort, was finally satisfied.

Of course the greatest mass of settlers left no records at all. English, American, Scotch and Irish, they appear briefly in the observations of

others. The British-born and those of British background looked
suspiciously at the Americans, associating them with dangerous
republican leanings and deploring their brash, insistent egalitarianism
of manner. Susanna Moodie is first amused, then appalled by her
borrowing neighbours; slatternly and unscrupulous Betty Fye was a
constant free-booter in her demands, totally lost to shame and almost
untouchable by fear: "I used to swear mighty big oaths till about a
month ago, when the Methody parson told me that if I did not have
it off I should go to a tarnation bad place; so I dropped some of the
worst of them."[16] And Old Satan, "disgustingly ugly," who had lost
one eye in a quarrel—"It had been gouged out in a free fight, and the
side of his face presented a succession of horrible scars inflicted by the
teeth of his savage adversary"—liked nothing better than to abuse the
British, insolently, to their faces. "The Yankees had whipped them,
and would whip them again. He was not afear'd of them, he never was
afear'd in his life."[17] These were the squatter types, the drifters whose
eyes were on the main chance and whose very presence seemed an
impediment to the country's progress. Sometimes, however, perhaps
quite often, their children climbed higher into self-respect and self-
support from their parents' squalid shiftlessness.

Scottish, Irish and English settlers, in all gradations and combina-
tions of active and potential skill and determination, hope and desperation, pressed into the opening rural areas. Sometimes, after about
sixteen years, like the Campbell family, settled among other Highlanders under the rough, demanding "protection" of Thomas Talbot,
they could be said to prosper:

One part of the country through which I passed today is settled chiefly
by Highlanders, who bring hither all their clannish attachments, and
their thrifty, dirty habits—and also their pride and their honesty. We
stopped about noon at one of these Highland settlements.... The
house was called Campbell's Inn, and consisted of a log-hut and a
cattle shed.... The family spoke nothing but Gaelic; a brood of
children, ragged, dirty, and without shoes or stockings ... were running about—and all stared upon me with a sort of half-scared, uncouth
curiosity which was quite savage.[18]

Irish immigrants who had known little self-respect and less hope
at home came over with nothing besides their vitality to commend
them. They had lived at the barest subsistence level in Ireland and
that, in the forties, became starvation; many of them, minimally
civilized already, were readily brutalized by hard lives and drink; as

Carlyle in England ranted against their barbarities, so the better-off in Canada viewed them with disgust or fear, as "vicious, uneducated barbarians," ... "I shrank, with feelings almost akin to fear, from the hard-featured, sunburnt women as they elbowed rudely past me."[19] Quite soon however, a weighing tolerance modified revulsion and the Irish were seen as a pool of labour for all the jobs that needed doing so quickly. They came over in steerage by the hundreds and the thousands and in the cholera years of the early thirties they died in appalling numbers:

"Is your father yet alive?"
"Yes, he had land up in Adelaide."
"Is your mother alive?"
"No, she died of the cholera, coming over. You see the cholera broke out in the ship and fifty-three people died, one after t'other, and were thrown into the sea ... it was nothing but splash, splash all day long— first one, then another ... my father had some money to receive of his pension, but ... it soon went; and then he sold his silver watch, and that brought us on to York—that's Toronto now. And then there was a schooner provided by government to take us on board, and we had rations provided, and that brought us to Port Stanley, far below Port Talbot; and then they put us ashore, and we had to find our way, and pay our way, to Delaware, where our lot of land was that cost eight dollars; and then we had nothing left, nothing at all. There were nine hundred emigrants encamped about Delaware, no better off than ourselves."[20]

Many settlers failed to tame the land, sheer bad luck conspiring with temperamental incompatibility for pioneering or physical limitations to crumble all the hopes into bitter defeat:

"Do you live here?"
"Yes, I have a farm hard by—in the bush here."
"How large is it?"
"One hundred and forty acres."
"How much cleared?"
"Five or six acres—thereabout."
"How long have you been on it?"
"Five years."
"And only five acres cleared? That is very little in five years. I have seen people who had cleared twice that quantity of land in half the time."
He replied, almost with fierceness, "Then they had money, or friends, or hands to help them; I have neither. I have in this wide world only myself! and set a man with only a pair of hands at one of them big

trees there! see what he'll make of it! You may swing the axe here from morning to night for a week before you let the daylight in upon you."[21]

Cheap rot-gut whiskey was the quickest means to blotting out the disappointment and the desperation. The spectacle of sodden, ugly drunkenness was as familiar to all those who lived in Upper Canada as to all those who wrote of it. Long before the anti-drink crusade gathered momentum and the "Temperance Movement" picked up moral force, observers and recorders were, one and all, appalled by the destruction and the waste of human resources in Upper Canada from the drinking of raw whiskey. It was poison and degradation to the Indians whose ruined culture was of very little support to them; they had been tragically caught a long time before between their own world and life-patterns, which they could not keep, and the white man's world and culture which they could not really enter. And now most of the remnants of tribes in the Southern part of the province were what they looked to be—miserable, degraded and disease-ridden.

A gentleman described to me a family of Mohawk Indians, consisting of seven individuals, who had encamped upon some of his uncleared land in two wigwams. They had made their first appearance in the early spring, and had since subsisted by hunting, selling their venison for whiskey or tobacco; their appearance and situation were, he said, most wretched, and their indolence extreme. Within three months, five out of the seven were dead of consumption; two only were left— languid, squalid, helpless, hopeless, heartless.[22]

Though the Indians and the poorest white settlers, almost without hope or self-respect anyhow, were most brutalized by whiskey, every level of society and all the people in it felt its effects. Where the labourer in England commonly drank ale, the Canadian labourer, at a barn-raising for instance, refreshed himself with a dipper of whiskey. It was easily manufactured in Canada, it was cheap—for decades no more than twenty-five cents a gallon—and, as long as the physique could stand it, it was the quick, easy and available path to an illusion of warmth, well-being—and oblivion. In a day when heavy drinking was commonplace and gentlemen who were "elated" began to forfeit respect only when they became flagrantly anti-social, Upper Canada was notorious for drunkenness. Whiskey, "unquestionably the greatest evil, . . . the vice and curse of this country," bitterly named "Canadian nectar," was as proportionate an agent for man's self-destruction in Upper Canada as gin had been in its eighteenth-century English hey- day.

Nothing in this heaving, straining picture, all scattered fragments and jagged edges, could possibly be called quiescent, much less stagnant. A mass of heterogeneous elements, yoked together by time, place and chance, fluctuating and wavering towards some rational, possible political and social identity, the province needed all kinds of ministrations at once. There were factors of balance in British rule and British traditions, in an ideal of a British-ordered social system, and in just as strong an America-derived ideal which issued, spoken and unspoken, in a "Jack's as good as his master" frame of mind.

There was the persistent tantalizing Crusoe-dream that resides in all men and haunts the pioneer, of a man's making his present and assuring his future all alone, by his own efforts. Like Crusoe, like Katie's Malcolm in his aspiration, such a man would be a Hero in Eden, isolated and alone to be sure, but preferring it so. He was threatened only by other people, not by nature, which he dreamed of dominating and quite often did dominate by his will and intelligence.[23] Physical circumstances and the nineteenth-century ritual-celebration of self-help and *laissez-faire* reinforced that dream, of course. Many men failed but more succeeded, though the price they paid was very great—often the loss, for a generation or more, of any meaning in life beyond the taming of a plot of unresponsive land in a tough climate.

There was also the counteracting impulse and straining towards social order, permanence and patterns of decorum. The vast majority of settlers of whatever stage or status believed—if only because they had to believe in order to live without despairing—in progress; they hoped for and as they worked towards physical and economic security and order, they also looked for security and order in society and within the walls of organized religion, to protect, to confine and to confirm their confidence in a God-ordered world. All the religions, all the sects were at work in Upper Canada, but the Methodists were the busiest missionaries and the most systematic "in their modes of declamation, as in their plans of church government. They are the same in every place . . . .[24]

As in Wesley's England, the people were especially ready for fervent evangelicalism and for Methodism's organization and ordered rules. Theirs was an Old Testament experience but later in time and diffused in purpose and expression, it was not as in earlier New England, accompanied by a powerful, sustaining vision of themselves as a latter-day Children of Israel. As physically, their pioneer experience was less fraught with drama and with danger, so spiritually, their comprehension of themselves and God was an altogether drabber, bleaker and humbler one than the Puritans' had been. They feared God or were at least very vulnerable to fear of Him—why not? Certainly everything that they found in their pioneer experience would confirm the doctrine of an angry God who required hard service before rejoicing, as the land demanded battle and did not repay love. Love of God? that was something far more remote. Man's duty on this earth was to repent, to fear God, and to work—always to work; God's privilege was to bestow love and a sense of His love. And sometimes, quite often in fact, the Methodist preacher, with his fervent prayings and exhortings, his assurance that work was, indeed, holy in the eyes of God, was the only agent in between. Particularly in the excitement of a Camp Meeting occasion, hundreds and hundreds of settlers would, for a little while, rejoice:

The writer [John Carroll], will never forget the impression made on his boyish imagination by the conversion of a whole band or tribe of Indians in a few hours, which he had the happiness to witness.... The Methodists of York and Yonge Street had prepared for a great camp meeting near Cummer's Mill. The Indians from the Credit turned out to a man, woman and child. A band of pagans, also, from the shores of Lake Simcoe somewhere, had heard that their brethren had found something which made them 'glad in their hearts'.... When the horn sounded for preaching they came pouring out of their camp. The old, bald-headed chief led the van, followed first by his warriors, and then by the women and children. They seated themselves on the left of the "preachers' stand," prepared for the Indians, surrounded by converted ones of other tribes....

Solemnity sat upon every face from the first. But soon the head of the old chief, and then of one and another was bowed in penitential sorrow, while tears channeled down the cheeks of those who had never wept before. Soon the power from above seemed greater and the agitation stronger; quaking, trembling, falling, were seen all through the Indian congregation. The preacher's voice was drowned with strong cries and shouts of joy from the liberated. He ceased, and a prayer meeting began which lasted with very little intermission till morning, and the whole of the pagans were happily converted to God.[25]

One of these, John Sunday, left his own story of the great occasion:

So we have pray meeting. None of us had religion yet. ... I saw one man and one woman shouting; I thought they were drunk. I thought this, they cannot be drunk, because is them Christian; must be something in them. . . . By and by the good Lord he pour his spirit upon my poor wretched heart: then I shout and happy in my heart. . . . I look around—and look over other side a Bay—and look up—and look in the woods; the same is everything NEW to me. I hope I got religion that day. I thank the great spirit what he done for me. I want to be like this which built his house upon a rock.[26]

With a perfection of simplicity, the children of the Credit Indian converts sang this hymn at York the next year; with perfect ceremonial approval, it was received:

> I could not read, I could not sew,
> My Saviour's name I did not know
> My parents oft I disobeyed,
> And to the Lord I never pray'd.
>
> The white man to the forest came,
> And taught the Indian Jesu's name;
> He built the church, the school-house rear'd,
> And holy hymns the dark wood cheer'd.
>
> I *now* can read, I *now* can sew,
> My Saviour's name I'm taught to know;
> And now my Saviour, I implore
> To bless the white man evermore.[27]

Then there was no cynicism on either side, nor any impact of stunning irony. In its time and place, the woeful tangling of the threads of the pattern was quite obscured from the comprehension of all parties.

Egerton Ryerson, who was preaching on the Yonge Street circuit in 1825-6, was present at this Camp Meeting. The first one to be held so near the town of York, no one within its range could ignore it completely. Whether to consider it an opportunity for salvation and an occasion for the outpouring of God's grace, an unseemly, pitiable or ludicrous spectacle, a dangerous emotional rallying point for the lower classes, or a shocking and immoral orgy, was determined by religious and social affiliations, attitudes and degrees of sophistication:

As you entered the ground, it sloped downward from the front gate to the "Preacher's stand," with "tent" attached, which stood at the other side of the area. The seats for the congregation (of new slabs from the mill) consequently rose with a gentle elevation from the stand; and they were prepared with a view to accommodate a vast number. The ground, though thoroughly cleared of small trees and rubbish, was delightfully shaded by the wide-spreading branches and thick foliage of the straight and towering forest trees that are left standing. The whole of the cleared space was encompassed with a strong fence *eight* or *ten* feet high, made of slabs. . . . sharpened at the top. . . . Each of the openings for egress and ingress, whether for food, water, or retirement, as well as the main entrance, particularly the latter, were furnished with gates strongly framed together, and secured by strong pins and massive bars. These were carefully guarded by a strong "watch," a sort of camp-meeting police, that relieved each other at intervals, and kept watch and ward the live-long night.[28]

Prominent inside the camp-palisade was the penitents' "pen" roughly sketched in with logs, close to the preacher's stand, the very heart of the ritual. There those whose hearts, like Wesley's, "were strangely warmed" by the preaching, the fervent exhortings and the singing, came forward from the congregation to pray and to be prayed over, until, hopefully, they "felt the power" and emotionally released, floating free of time and place, they saw "the resurrection and the light."[29] Preaching and singing worked in tandem to whip their hearers into quaking fear and to soothe them into hope. A soul-shaking sermon on doom and judgment on the text "And I saw a great white throne, and Him that sat on it, from whose face the earth and the heaven fled away; and there was found no place for them," would be followed by the wailing cadences of the Dies Irae:

> Day of wrath! O day of mourning!
> See fulfilled the prophet's warning—
> Heaven and earth in ashes burning!
>
> Ah that day of tears and mourning!
> From the dust of earth returning,
> Man for judgment must prepare him
> Spare, O God, in mercy spare him![30]

Then as the listeners became more agitated, the preachers and the confident believers would exhort them to repentance, several would pray in turn or, indeed, two or three at once; the mourner's bench or penitents' pen would fill with shaken sinners, and the simple, familiar revival hymns would swell out, all up the emotional scale in easy words and bouncing rhythm, from despair:

> O there'll be mourning, mourning, mourning,
>   mourning
> At the judgment seat of Christ,

to supplication:

> I'm a-rolling, I'm a-rolling, I'm a-rolling
> Through an unfriendly world;
> O brothers, won't you help me?
> O brothers, won't you help me to pray?
> Won't you help me in the service of the Lord?

and finally to glad release:

> O brothers, will you meet us
> On Canaan's heavenly shore?
> O brothers, will you meet us
> Where parting is no more?

> *Chorus:* Then we'll march around Jerusalem
> We'll march around Jerusalem
> We'll march around Jerusalem
> When we arrive at home.[31]

Although the strong walls, the barred gates and the watch were usually protection enough against louts and smart-alecs, looking for easy fights or women, they were no protection against the piercing eye of the "polite" public which bored through them easily and saw in imagination, unmentionable profligacy. There was certainly hysteria at the Camp Meetings; there were certainly excesses and all the vulgarity that the reserved and the refined could dream to sniff at. The ignorant man who prayed, "Make us, good Lord, like Sodom and Gomorrow," and the listener who refused to say "Amen," because "Sodom and Gomorrow were two very wicked men,"[32] may have been matched in hundreds. However, fifty years on the mellow memories of the good grey preachers insisted on the dignity of the Camp Meetings' accomplishment. Building a palisade of sharpened stakes for the worship of a God of love did not seem strange to them; in their time and place, to their habit of mind, it was not strange. Had not Paradise itself required walls, a gate and a watch? And undoubtedly, the Camp Meetings were *great occasions* among a people who needed every kind of recreation, of security, and of reassurance, social and spiritual: "The effect of such meetings is to promote acquaintance and brotherly love between all the church, both ministers and members: and to check a tendency to secularism and to promote heavenly-mindedness. The writer [John Carroll] remembers the regret he felt at going back into the world after the meeting was over."[33]

"For why?" they sang as they left, in the cornerstone hymn they called the "Old Hundred":

> For why? The Lord our God is good;
> His mercy is forever sure;
> His truth at all times firmly stood;
> And shall from age to age endure.

And that, those angular words, to a tune as tough and hard and plodding as their lives had made the settlers who sang it, affirmed for them their world's extra and indispensable dimension—of faith and of the spirit.

Chapter 4

Ryerson and Strachan: The Beginnings of Controversy

Egerton Ryerson had grown up in a relatively favoured position in this raw Upper Canadian world, where so many of the settlers were either the deprived or the desperate poor, and where most children were schooled sketchily, sporadically, barbarically, or not at all. Though all the leaders knew the need and recognized the hope for social coherence in the future through education, there were, in the early twenties, only a handful of competent schools, either state supported or private. Educated emigrants who settled out of range of these had to accept one of the worst of the disappointments of a new land, the knowledge that their children could not be educated to their parents' level, much less above it. And ignorant emigrants were often apathetic or even hostile to the idea of education for their children, as a seduction of their labour force.

Long before, Governor Simcoe had begun the system of public education, recommending the founding of Grammar Schools in each of the official districts of Upper Canada and the granting of funds for their upkeep. To his mind, the colony also required a university: "Liberal education seems to me to be indispensably necessary; and the completion of it by the establishment of a university in the Capital of the Country . . . would be most useful to inculcate just principles, habits and manners among the rising generation. . . ."[1] Both the university and the entire embryonic school system had long since begun to figure as ripe political bones, to be worried and gnawed at by the viciously factional parties with as much joy in battle as in progress, and "Clergy Reserves" for decades the war cry.

Ryerson was initiated into the endemic religious-political-educational controversy in the year after his entrance into the Methodist

Ministry. Though he protested, privately at least, that pamphleteering often caused him "leanness of soul," he proved the most able and articulate controversialist among the Methodists; if he truly deplored the battles, he did certainly enjoy the exercises of strategy in his engagements.

In 1824, the first year of his ministry, he was appointed to the York and Yonge Street circuit. "I travel about two hundred miles in four weeks, and preach twenty-five times, besides funerals."[2] Two Sundays a month he was in the country and two Sundays in York, where about fifty of the thousand inhabitants formed the congregation in the Methodist Chapel on King Street. The town was a strange, rough amalgam of provincial capital, army garrison and crude frontier village, still carrying a certain stigma as a compromise capital. The governor and troops, however competent and however loyal, had only a temporary stake in the country and the few leading families, traditionally Tory and Anglican, were as confident of their own enlightenment as their opposition rapidly became convinced of their self-interest. Around these none-too-stable centres milled the energies, the dreams and drives and necessities of an emigrant population that grew to ten thousand in ten years, constantly straining to the limits the abilities of a new young community to cope with its own development.

Ryerson enjoyed preaching in York. Neither the prayer, the meditation, nor the confessional of his diary could eradicate, to his spiritual satisfaction, his thirsting "too ardently for the honours of the world."[3] And though he rejoiced in his diary that he had been spared from vanity and pride, he retained a very healthy appreciation of his own efforts and his own abilities and a healthy pleasure in any confirmation of his own confidence: "In York we have most flattering prospects. . . . Our morning congregation fill the chapel, which was never the case before; and in the evening the chapel will not contain but little more than three-quarters of the people. Last evening, several members of Parliament were present."[4]

Out of civic interest, but certainly impelled also by a personal attraction towards debate, he spent time in the Legislature where he could scarcely fail to feel himself at least as competent as most of the representatives he heard. He had read and studied Blackstone's Commentaries on the laws of England, especially the rights of the Crown, and Parliament and Subject, and Paley's Moral and Political Philosophy; "and when I read and observed the character of the policy, and state of things in Canada, I felt that it was not according to the principles of British liberty, or of the British Constitution. . . ."[5]

In January of 1826, his presence as preacher in York, was re-marked and approved by William Lyon Mackenzie, in the *Colonial Advocate*. Ryerson's partner and senior on the circuit was the Rev. James Richardson, but it is Ryerson who is singled out for praise as Mackenzie reviews the Methodist service:

It is of great advantage to a preacher when he has read much and studied much, not only in the sacred scriptures, but also in that vast record of human perseverance, miscellaneous literature. And that Mr. Ryerson has not been negligent in this respect, is apparent from the tenor of his discourses . . . .
N.B. We were all pleased to see Mr. Rolph, the Hon. the Speaker [Bidwell], and many others who were in the Presbyterian Church in the afternoon, in the Wesleyan Church in the evening—this is a beginning of the times when such distinctions shall be done away, and the term Christian alone remain.[6]

If saying could only have made it so, Mackenzie would certainly have reformed the Christian church, along with all bad government and every darkness that corrupts the human condition. He was already ardently poking, prodding and igniting the Upper Canadian scene wherever he could, and his approval and praise were to be valued.

However, the strongest, busiest man of ecclesiastical affairs in York, John Strachan, Archdeacon, did not acknowledge the legal existence of the Methodists, much less noticing their promising young minister. Like Mackenzie, Strachan was a Scot who had come to Upper Canada with ambition and the potential for its realiza-tion. But unlike the burning reformer-zealot, uneasily balanced between hysteria and genius, forever illusioned by Utopian dreams and forever disappointed, Strachan built steadily towards the stability of a conservative social order. He moved confidently out from his cornerstone conviction, "that the establishment is formed, not for the purpose of making the Church political, but for the purpose of making the State religious."[7] A convert from the Presbyterian church to the Anglican, Strachan carried with him the special sense of mission of a zealous convert, the toughness of mind of his Calvin-istic heritage, and an enormous confidence, energy and strength of intellect and personality that made him a natural leader and a most formidable opponent.

The Grammar School which he began to build up at Cornwall, in 1803, was certainly the first distinguished school in Upper Canada. Its headmaster had, neither then nor later, in his own eyes or in the opinions of the leading Anglican families of the colony, any rival as the colony's educational pundit. His removal from Cornwall to York carried with it a solidly-established reputation, but his conduct during "The American War" wove around him a special aura of moral and physical courage which he then earned and afterwards maintained.

He was ready to be a battling clergyman, in fact and in spirit; shortly after the declaration of war, he and his family were on a ship in the St. Lawrence which was threatened by an approaching schooner, believed to be American and armed. The Canadian captain was ready to surrender, but Strachan sent him down to the cabin and prepared himself to command the defence of the ship with its one four-pounder cannon. He enjoyed recounting the incident later: "Fortunately for me, the schooner bearing down upon us proved to be a Canadian schooner, not an American; for the four-pounder was fastened to the deck, and it pointed to the starboard whereas the schooner came to us on the larboard bow."[8]

His finest moment came, however, with the attack on York in 1813 and its distraught sequel. The Americans' "capture" of the fort was far more an establishment of their presence than a battle, for the small defending force was totally confused and demoralized. But in the panicky aftermath the garrison's magazine was blown up with a great loss of life. Among the dead was the American general, Pike. When, in retaliation, York was threatened with burning, out from the town as its emissary rode John Strachan, his black cape flying behind him in his speed, but no tremor of panic disturbing either his conviction of the right, or his confidence in his own power to make it, in this case, prevail. According to witnesses "words ran high" between General Dearborn and John Strachan, but "the earnestness and determination of Dr. Strachan moved the General from his barbarous purpose, and York was saved from the flames."[9]

Such leadership neither died in the memories of the town, nor in the self-esteem and confidence of John Strachan. To it was joined over the years a tireless energy of social service and charity in visiting the poor, the sick and the prisoners, climaxing in really heroic endeavour during the cholera epidemics of the thirties, when he, in his mid-fifties, was minister, nurse and undertaker. In the summer of 1832 about fifty thousand emigrants landed at Quebec and four-fifths of them came on to Upper Canada. At best they were usually penniless after the six-hundred-mile journey; this year epidemic was added to poverty. In the fall, after the worst was over, Strachan wrote to a friend:

The terrible disease attacked them as they journeyed hither; many died on the way; others were landed in various stages of the disease; and many were seized after they came among us. In short, York became one general hospital. We had a large building fitted up comfortably for the reception of the cholera patients; but the cases were so numerous that many could not be conveyed to it, and remained at their own houses, or lodgings. It is computed that one in four of the adults of this town were attacked, and that one-twelfth of the whole population died.[10]

John Strachan's conception of duty admitted neither fear nor faltering. He had only one clerical assistant and that young man, after surviving an attack of cholera became understandably nervous about visiting the sick and dying in the hospital. Strachan carried on alone:

. . . Often have I been in the malignant ward, with six or eight expiring around me. The foulness of the air, too, was at times overpowering; but I always, by the blessing of God, found my nerves equal to the occasion, and it seems as if this summer I was stronger than usual, and fully equal to the increase of labour thrown upon me. The disease has now almost entirely ceased; but it has left many blanks in our society, and, what is still more painful, about one hundred widows and four hundred children,—all strangers in a strange land, and dependent upon the charity of those amongst whom the Providence of God has thrown them.[11]

The many strengths of this man diffused themselves in the growth of York and the entire province; their forcing effect is nowhere more marked than in the swift development of Egerton Ryerson, from a pious, raw young minister of promise, to a decisive, confident and seasoned controversialist.

Strachan had an abiding dream, of Upper Canada as a little England:

In imagination, Dr. Strachan beheld a noble Province, divided into parallelograms and apportioned into parishes, each parish the centre of an accredited representative of that genial, well-mannered Christianity which is the popular characteristic of the Clergy of the rational Church; the settled abode of one whose character would be respected and whose influence would be seen in the everyday intercourse of common life. His desire was that religion and learning, re-acting on one another, should sanctify taste, elevate morals, purify manners, and blend with the hard and roughening influences of the backwoods, many of the social refinements and home attractions which grow around the old grey Church towers and within the trim parsonage of England. The vision of Church work through the whole of its educational course, from the cradle to the grave, formed in his mind a vision of present loveliness and future peace.[12]

Both the people and the land itself defeated Strachan's dream. To him, physical and geographical difficulties were challenges, not obstacles: in his years of teaching at Cornwall, a forty- or fifty-mile missionary trip among settlements along the St. Lawrence had been a holiday. In middle age, he would go ten miles up to Hogg's Hollow on a Sunday in a heavy rain, when perhaps he might find only one parishioner waiting to hear him preach. But the land imposed its own realities and its own necessities. It was too rough, distances were too great, seasonal variations in the weather were too sudden and violent for the development of Southern England's pleasant pattern of reassurance in hedgerow and cropped field, village and church spire. more than that, Upper Canada's immigrant population, though mostly bound by choice to English institutions, increasingly pushed towards the largest measure obtainable of self-determination within the smallest confinement possible of protective paternalism.

Egerton Ryerson understood the quality of the land and its imposing of its own conditions, not with an acquired knowledge, but essentially, bone-deep, as his father had known better how to clear and farm his holdings because of experience bred-in, after generations in North America. Ryerson knew too, and shared, the temper of mind: he was conservative in temperament and proud of his family's Loyalist tradition, but that very pride contained a resistance to a British shadow-colony and an undefined but developing insistence on a uniquely North American adaptation of British institutions to the Upper Canadian scene. He was also a Methodist by conviction and by choice, eagerly ready to defend his church.

On July 3, 1825, John Strachan delivered a sermon on the death of Dr. Mountain, the Bishop of Quebec. Since 1822, the Church of Scotland, claiming recognition as an Established Church, had been making strong claims for a portion of the Clergy Reserves' resources. John Strachan was vitally interested in refuting its argument; his sermon was in large part for British, not for North American, eyes and ears. It was printed in the spring of 1826, as Strachan prepared to go to England to seek a University Charter. In the sermon, he generally cried woe upon the state of the Anglican church in America, upon the uneducated dissenting Clergymen of all sects who were too often the people's only ministrants, and particularly upon the Methodists. In Strachan's earnestly-argued opinion, only the addition of a large money grant to the complete use of the vast Clergy Reserve tracts in Upper Canada could put the Established Church where it must be, to fulfil its enormous duty in the civilizing of the whole colony.

Just a year after his saddle-bag beginning, at a monthly social and prayer-meeting in York, Ryerson heard the pamphlet-sermon of the Archdeacon and was charged by his fellow-Methodists to write something in their defence. Looking back, he speaks with ritual modesty of his unworthiness and unwillingness; in fact, he had certainly every reason to be daunted at the prospect of engaging in battle against John Strachan. He had also the consciousness that his educational training was laughably incomplete by Strachan's standards, and the knowledge that his rebuttal, if less than effective, would be used as evidence that the Methodists were what Strachan said they were—a set of ignorant ranters, likely to do the State and the people more harm than good. But he also had both confidence and ambition—a year on circuit had strengthened his devotion to Methodism; it had also sent him driving toward something more than circuit-riding as his contribution and career.

James Richardson and Ryerson were both asked to write a reply to Strachan during their next circuit trip, but in a month, at the next group meeting in York, it was "the Boy Preacher," as they called him, who had a ten-thousand-word reply ready. When they heard it, the group members were certainly confirmed in their growing feeling that Egerton Ryerson was something special in their midst. When printed, "the Review," as it was called, caused a first class boil-up in tight little York and the hinterlands: "Its publication produced a sensation scarcely less violent and general than a Fenian invasion. It is said that before every house in Toronto might be seen groups reading and discussing the paper on the evening of its publication in June; and the excitement spread throughout the country. It was the first defiant defence of the Methodists, and of the equal and civil rights of all religious persuasions."[13]

The mouse had roared at the lion—and with good effect. Within two weeks, there were four answers to the Review in the press, calling its writer an ignoramus, a crafty politician, a rebel and a traitor, and a "proud boaster of his learning." However, Ryerson's friends and supporters admired the quality of his defiance as much as his words themselves, though even they were sometimes tempted to describe his flouting of the Establishment as rash, even arrogant. As

for his family, his clergy brothers cheered, but with certain caution-
ary admonitions, and his father finally confronted him with the question: " 'Egerton, they say that you are the author of these papers which
are convulsing the whole country. I want to know whether you are
or not?' And when the answer was 'yes,' my Father lifted up his
hands in an agony of feeling, and exclaimed, 'My God! we are all
ruined!' "[14] Ryerson himself felt that he must "either flee or fight. I
decided upon the latter . . . devoted a day to fasting and prayer, and
then went at my adversaries in good earnest."[15] He was unshakeably
sure of the righteousness of the Methodist cause and besides competence, he had also the brashness in challenge that his older colleagues
lacked.

"The Review" is a remarkably effective piece of argumentative
rhetoric, doubly so read as the maiden effort of a self-taught young
man in battle with Upper Canada's senior religious and educational
figure. Ryerson dissects Strachan's argument point after point, ham-
mering home his rebuttals with a skill in the traditional rhetorical
devices which would be impressive in a parliamentarian or a preacher
of twice his age and training. The fine blade of irony and the solid
buttressing by authority are his best tools:

We are sorry to see the Doctor reduced to such a dilemma of agitation and distress; but we fear his recovery will not be immediate.
He asks, in the language of despair, "What can fifty-three clergymen
do, scattered over a country of greater extent than Great Britain?"
For the Doctor's reflection and encouragement I would ask, "What
did twelve apostles do in the midst of an obstinate, barbarous and per-
secuting world? What did a Waldus do in the valleys of Piedmont?
What did a Wycliffe do in England? What did a Luther do in
Germany; nay, in the Christian world? What did a Wesley and his
contemporaries do in Europe? What have the Methodists done in
America?" The most of these were not endowed with miraculous
gifts. Why did *they* not cry out in the tone of discouragement, "What
can one man do in the face of an anti-Christian world?" Why did *they*
not apply to some Legislature for pecuniary aid? Simply because they
had learned that "the race is not to the swift nor the battle to the
strong."[16]

What both sides had often thought, but ne'er so well expressed, was
now in the open, a burning controversy in the press and the subject of
a thousand private conversations and arguments. It was to be discussed in session after heated session in Parliament, both in Canada
and England, a prime political issue and a cornerstone of each faction's

platform, through and far beyond the Rebellion. Not until 1854 was the Clergy Reserves question finally settled—and then to no one group's complete satisfaction, but with the legal equality of all religions finally established.

The organization, rules and Discipline of the Methodists, particularly its pattern of yearly change for its preachers were all well-designed to nip a young man's growth of undue pride in controversial skill, or in any other area of his duties. At the Conference of 1826, Ryerson was appointed Missionary to the Credit River Indians, at the same time sharing the preaching in York with his brother William. About two hundred Chippewas lived, or existed on the barest subsistence level, on a tract of land beside the Credit, twelve miles to the west of York. The government had built a group of cabins for them and proposed also to erect a church—an Anglican church of course, where the blessings and the sacraments of the Lord would be dispensed hand in hand with the benign patronage of "the Great White Father," George IV.

From its very beginning, Methodism's strongest strain had been missionary; now the Credit River situation presented a double opportunity—to extend the preaching and influence of the Methodist church and to score a goal ahead of the Church of England. Fifty years later the defensiveness of early Canadian Methodists and the intensity of their rivalry with the Establishment were still fresh and strong to Ryerson. Reminiscing in the seventies, he rejoiced doubly that he, of impeccable Loyalist descent, had been appointed "as the first stationed Missionary among the Indians . . . standing proof that the imputation of disloyalty against the Methodist Missionaries was groundless," and that he had resolved to be ahead of the Anglicans in building a church. "I called the Indians together on the Monday morning after the first Sunday's worship with them, and using the head of a barrel for a desk, commenced a subscription among them to build a house for the double purpose of the worship of God and the teaching of their children."[17]

The self-examining, analytic mind of the twentieth century finds in the motivations, the methods and the results of nineteenth-century missions a jungle ripe for the hacking and hewing of its skeptical research. Certainly Canadian Methodists operated from as shaky a platform of conviction compounded with naïvete as any other missionaries, and their incidence of human error was as great. Only a handful of white men on the entire continent began to understand, as did Henry Schoolcraft of Michilimackinac, the cultural reality of the nomadic tribes, and no one offered their people acceptance with dignity and without either cynical exploitation or well-meant, officious, useless meddling. Besides, in 1825 in Upper Canada, the time was late: the fabric of Indian culture was rotten and a little group like the Credit Chippewas, demoralized and disease-ridden, were a constant cumulative menace to themselves and to others. The question was how much human dignity and potential value could be saved from the wreck.

To the missionary-preacher, the heathen saved and redeemed were the prime and urgent challenge, but a man like Egerton Ryerson, still impatiently young and strong, was bound to find special satisfaction in a job demanding a whole range of skills and showing quick returns in practical success for his efforts. The Credit Indians were still living in their bark-covered and brush-enclosed wigwams when he arrived. He lived in one of them for several weeks, "my bed consisting of a plank, a mat and a blanket, and a blanket also for my covering; yet I was never more comfortable and happy.... I showed the Indians that I could work and live as they worked and lived."[18]

He used the skills of his farm background among them, supervising the building of his church-school, showing the Indians how to clear and fence, plough and plant their first wheat and corn-fields. In two weeks, he learned to understand Mississauga and shortly to speak it. He helped teach in the school of about forty Indian children. With Peter Jones, an Indian convert who was highly regarded among the Methodist hierarchy and influential among his own people, he travelled to other settlements in the province, and to the Annual Indian assembly at Holland Landing where the government bounties were distributed. After this tour, Ryerson presented himself to Sir Peregrine Maitland, the Lieutenant-Governor, carrying a report on the progress of the Methodist Christianizing, civilizing and educating mission among the Indians. His report also contained a petition for their present and future protection from unscrupulous, exploiting, whiskey-dispensing traders, predictably and bitterly denounced in his report as "Roman Catholic Frenchmen ... who are violently opposed to the reformation of the Indians."[19]

All of this was violent, demanding, quickly successful and satisfying physical activity for a young man of twenty-three. There was also a "tenderness in the disposition" of the Chippewas which drew Ryerson to them. They were a gentle, kind, teachable and malleable people when not wild from drink or completely broken and dejected in spirit:

I have this week been trying to procure for the Indians the exclusive right of their salmon fishery, which I trust will be granted by the Legislature. I have attended one of their Councils, where everything was conducted in the most orderly manner.... The old Chief arose, and approached the table where I was sitting, and in his own tongue addressed me in the following manner: "Brother, as we are brothers, we will give you a name. My departed brother was named Chuhock; thou shalt be called Chuhock."[20]

And brother William, visiting the settlement with the combined attitudes of friendly brother and Inspector-General, reported his approval to brother George. That Egerton was "almost worshipped by his people" held nothing to him of a pitiful, mistaken, man-for-God identification, equally dangerous to the giver and the receiver. The whole mission seemed, in his eyes, a great success:

I was highly delighted to see the improvement they are making both in religious knowledge and industry.... On my arrival at the Mission I found Egerton about half a mile from the village stripped to the shirt and pantaloons, clearing land with between twelve and twenty of the little Indian boys, who were all engaged in chopping and picking up the brush. It was an interesting sight. Indeed he told me that he spent an hour or more every morning and evening in this way, for the benefit of his own health and the improvement of the Indian children. He is almost worshipped by his people....[21]

The preacher-brothers, George, William and John, acted, both bidden and unbidden, as counsellors and mentors for Egerton. William preached most eloquently of all of them; at this time he was closest to the centre of Methodist practice and policy. When Egerton faltered in the pamphlet-controversy with the Anglicans that was continuing sporadically through these years, complaining that he felt like "a target to be shot at by everyone," William gave him heart—and sound advice:

I send you a pamphlet containing Dr. Strachan's defence before the Legislative Council. If I had time I would write a reply, at least to a part of it. I think you had better write a full answer to it.... If you write a full answer would it not be better to do it in the form of letters, addressed to the doctor, and signed by your real name? Write in a candid, mild, and kindly style, and it will have a much more powerful effect upon the mind of the public. Do not cramp yourself, but write fully, seriously, and effectually.[22]

John could be just as forthright and explicit in his advice. However, his bluntness seldom, if ever, carried the hint of elder-brother patronage and conscious seniority that William's did: he was closest to

Egerton in age, he was more tactful than William, and he and Egerton had a particular warmth of affection for each other. It was John who, in his highly individual spelling and grammar, advised oftenest on personal matters—at this point in his brother's life, on marriage.

Hannah Aikman and Egerton had been attracted to each other in 1824 before his entry into the ministry, when he lived at her father's house in Hamilton overworking himself into a breakdown at John Law's school. The two had an understanding, but Hannah released Egerton from any responsibility to her when he entered the Ministry. In economic terms, marriage then was impossible; a circuit rider had no home and almost no income. The conference could only afford to pay fifty dollars a year when Ryerson began and for food and lodging the preacher depended on the goodwill and charity of his widely-dispersed flock.

Though impelled by conviction towards the ministry, Ryerson would certainly have been goaded by his own ambition and the consciousness of his own powers towards advancement to the top of any profession which he had chosen. In 1828, when he was switched from the Credit Indian Mission to the Cobourg circuit, he was no longer a probationer, but a seasoned preacher with three years of experience behind him. He was also a prime agent in the rising stock of Upper Canadian Methodism and now he could afford to think of marrying. "My ministerial friends all advise me now to marry," he wrote in his diary. Their advice must have included some assurance of financial solvency.

Egerton had annoyed his brother John by some piece of shilly-shallying regarding Hannah and she, meanwhile, had entered into a brief engagement with the youngest Ryerson, Edwy, who was still at home on the farm. In January of 1828 brother John poured a stiff dose of medicine for the lovesick and foolish:

The instability and indecision of character that you have manifested in this affare have not a little surprised me. I shall never give any more advise on subjects of this kind if I can help it, but as you wish for information with respect to one or two things, I would just say (though with reluctance) that my opinion, relating to Miss A's general character & qualifications, is the same that it has always been, *but* the haisty, inconsiderate & indisoluble engagements she made with Edwy I highly disapprove of & so must every person of sence. The correctness & propriety of her conduct in now breaking these promises I leave her own conscience to determon; but am of the opinion that had they of got married that neather of them would of been happy.... [23]

By September of 1828, troubles sorted and reconciled, Hannah and Egerton were married—by a Presbyterian. The Methodists could not yet legally perform marriages.

Hannah Ryerson figures in her husband's journals only as the conventional wife-and-mother figure of the pious nineteenth-century tradition. There is no trace of a living, breathing, differentiated human being in his eulogy of her virtues before marriage, or in the tribute he wrote her in 1833, a year after her death which shortly followed the birth of their second child. He represents her, as he does his mother, as all grace and dignity, without the matriarchal strength and force of character of a Susanna Wesley, but as a perfect helpmeet to her husband and an angelic influence on their children. There was no doubt a large measure of self-defence in this current and commonplace masking of the real woman in an angelic one: it became doubly comforting to insist on the essential importance of the spiritual journey in the face of the hazards attending the earthly journey of a child-bearing woman in a pioneer community.

In fact, of course, marriage visited Ryerson and Hannah with the excitements, the satisfactions and the frustrations that sexual adventure affords and that the human being demands, be he or she ever so committed to God and Methodism. The miracle of piety that he paints her incorporates, though unmemorialized, the Hannah Ryerson whose "fondness for me was extravagant," and Ryerson's three and a half years with "the wife of my youth" were a great and a happy adventure.

Chapter 5

Journalism and Diplomacy

Nothing in the history of Canadian Methodism gives firmer evidence of its energetic, opportunistic dynamism than the way in which its leaders showed awareness of Egerton Ryerson's growing capacities and exploited him, subject to their own discipline, at every turn. Strong physically and mentally and now comfortable in marriage and encouraged by approval, Ryerson throve on the growth-forcing process; for every recorded cry of weariness in controversy, there are a half-dozen evidences of intense satisfaction in the exercise of his mind and pen, particularly in playing Upper Canada's David to Strachan's Goliath.

At the conference of 1829, the Methodists decided to found a weekly publication called *The Christian Guardian*. In three years they had leaped from a position almost unworthy of notice by the Establishment, to become a powerful force in Upper Canada with about twelve thousand registered members, uncounted sympathizers, and a strong position to be maintained on the burning questions of the jurisdictions of Church, State and Education. It was time for them to enter the violently factional press warfare with their own voice; Ryerson's brief but intensive training in controversy and his quick response to the demands and the challenges of journalistic rhetoric made him their obvious choice.

They sent him off to New York, commissioned to buy a press and all its apparatus under Methodist auspices there, to print a paper "in defence of Methodist institutions and character, civil rights, temperance principles, educational progress and missionary operations."[1] Always functioning within a strong framework of discipline, the Methodists' driving impulse led them towards extending their ordering influence within a secular as well as a spiritual frame, to be in their

60

own sense every brother's keeper, and to watch and ward over the whole community. In the *Guardian*, Ryerson took all society's concerns as his province, with outstanding success. From the beginning he blandished the readers with a shrewd diversity of subject matter, from the traditional Almanac "how to do" instruction on everything from pest-control to the brewing of beer, to the equally traditional but more recently established content of the polite periodical for family reading. Articles on marriage and on home economy, eminently suitable literary excerpts, "A Chapter from the Life of Mr. John Wesley" for instance, intersperse the more serious concerns of Methodism— Missions, for instance, and the promotion of the "Temperance Movement" which had begun to sweep across the province quickly picking up the unrelenting pressure which pushed it beyond moderation to total abstinence.

The *Guardian's* respectable piety and the variety of its reader-interest were far outweighed in importance to serious members of the connexion by its weekly continuance of the battle for Methodism's place in the sun beside and not behind the Anglican church. Since the break-out of controversy, all the province's liberal, reform-minded or radical thinkers had approved the Methodist stand. But the support of Mackenzie, the most vocal and most committed of all the Reformers, sometimes proved unsettling at the least, and at most acutely embarrassing to Methodists. While insistent on a large degree of religious and civil liberty, there were few who were as reckless as he was, either of end results or of traditional decorums of life and manners. Now, with the *Guardian*, they expected to be heard in their own voice, their chosen editor responsible to the conference, speaking "the Methodist view" and walking somehow in balance, certainly reformers in action and spirit but never anarchists of the entire legal, political, or social structure.

Their severest critics and most dedicated opponents never censored the Methodists for lack of organization. Lieutenant-Governor Sir John Colborne, replying to the petition of the Conference of 1831, an argument for recognition and legal status, and against Anglican domination of university education, splendidly rationalized their aims in terms of their "efficacious" system:

Your dislike to any church establishment, or to the particular form of Christianity which is dominated by the Church of England, may be the natural consequence of the constant success of your own efficacious and organized system. The small number of our Church is to be regretted, as well as that the organization of its ministry is not adapted to supply the present wants of the dispersed population in this new country.... The utility of an Establishment depends entirely on the piety, assiduity, and devoted zeal of its ministers, and their abstaining from a secular interference which may involve them in political disputes.[2]

Colborne ended his reply with a sharp rebuke and a nasty cut to the area where the Methodists were most personally sensitive and vulnerable: "The system of University Education which has produced the best and ablest men in the United Kingdom will not be abandoned here to suit the limited views of the leaders of Societies who, perhaps, have neither experience nor judgment to appreciate the value or advantages of a liberal education...."[3]

Each side argued from a position of total conviction. Though in the popular mind Colborne and "the Family Compact" speedily became the villains of the piece, the representative of British government had good precedent to insist on Methodism as a "Society," as a "Connexion," with the Established Church its firm parent. Wesley himself had insisted on this. Officials could reasonably argue that the Canadian Methodists were arguing for autonomy after the precedent of the American church, which had happened by mistake as it were, and which, while it might well enjoy official recognition in another national state, was certainly not to be encouraged in a British colony.

Other sects followed the progress of Methodist battle with their own stakes in the outcome. Many Presbyterians, for example, whose clergy already shared official acceptance with the Anglicans, approved Ryerson's policy in the *Guardian*. One of their ministers complimented him—"some of your writings that I have seen discover both good sense and Christian feeling," and pledged support, his reasons a reflection of the feelings of many other members of widely differing sects. "The liberality, too, you have discovered, both in regard to myself and in regard of my brethren, has not escaped my observation. Be not discouraged by the malice of the enemies of religion. Your *Guardian* I have seldom seen but from this time I intend to take it regularly. Consider me one of your 'constant readers'. The matters in which we differ are nothing in comparison of those in which we agree."[4]

In his first three years as editor of the *Guardian,* Egerton Ryerson learned every practical detail of journalistic enterprise. Always operating on a shoe-string budget, he and his assistant, Franklin Metcalf, who was then the preacher at York, planned, wrote, solicited copy, shortly accepted advertising, looked after circulation and book-keeping, set type or trained others to do it, and produced a weekly which for its place and time demonstrated remarkably balanced, competent journalism. Ryerson's natural facility with the written word progressed to a first-class journalistic style, the tone and temper of it suited to the reader, but inducing a temperate balance in argument—a contrast to the spiralling intensity of Mackenzie's outpourings in the *Colonial Advocate*. From a beginning five hundred, the *Guardian's* subscription list rose by 1832 to nearly 3000. In these three years Methodism gained on all fronts. In 1831 the right of their clergy to perform marriages and burials was sanctioned by law, and in 1832 they opened Upper Canada Academy at Cobourg, for the training of their ministers.

Hannah Ryerson died shortly after the birth of her second child, in January of 1832. Various members of the family cared for John, a little boy of two, and the baby, Lucilla Hannah, while their father bore his bereavement with all the outward signs of the conventional acceptance of the will of God that ritually justified her death, but did not soothe his loss. Some comfort there was, perhaps, of a very cold kind, in being one of so many men whose wives died in childbirth. His brother George who had also been a widower, wrote to him: "I know how to feel for you, and you as yet know but a very small part of your trials. Years will not heal the wound. I am, even now, often quite overwhelmed when I allow myself to dwell upon the past."[5]

In August of 1832, Ryerson was released from his editorship to prepare for a journey to England to negotiate about a possible solution to Canadian Methodism's greatest internal threat—its situation with the British Wesleyans.[6] Preparing meant starting at the very practical beginning, with a tour of the province to gather money for his expenses. The question of the jurisdiction and authority of Canadian Methodists over their own concerns was ineradicably linked with politics and overall colonial policy. Back in England, Wesleyans were as convinced of their own duty to dominate where they could their Canadian brothers in Methodism, as they were honestly convinced of the drift toward republicanism of the Canadian conference. And they were certainly at least as convinced that it was politic and expedient to take this line by the state of their own reputation and funds in England.

The very dynamism and yeasty independence of Canada's Methodists made them subject to violent factional dispute among themselves; union with the British conference was for years as shattering an issue within as the Clergy Reserves were a rallying issue on the outside. Most of the people who were Methodists were simple and rural; the only theology, the only politics, and the only journalism they knew presented them with clear choices, heaven or hell, freedom or oppression, God or the Devil. On any occasion or subject presented, they chose up sides and battled with great doctrinaire enthusiasm; each side was convinced of its grasp of the truth and each man involved found some release from hard physical work and a certain degree of mental and emotional stimulation in factional battling for what seemed to be great and urgent causes.

Until this time George Ryerson had acted as the prime overseas diplomat of Canadian Methodism. He had been in England in the late twenties and now he was there again, concerned both with the settling of his wife's mother's family estate and with presenting the cause of Canadian Methodism to both government and British Wesleyan officials. George wrote dire warnings to Egerton about the British Wesleyans, particularly about the numbers of them who were enquiring about becoming preachers in Canada: "I notice they all enquire *first* and apparently with the most solicitude about the pecuniary part. . . . They have lost none of their primitive zeal, and this zeal is now whetted to the utmost keenness by the hardness of the times at 'home.' The Wesleyans have a very abundant share of this kind of men, & many *willing* to emigrate, as they will inform you (after making the more important preliminary enquiries), '*for the good of souls*'! But be warned and be sure you try the spirits."[7]

George was convinced himself of the purer Christian quality of Canadian Methodism, and he was smarting and defensive in a religious climate where he had received "much civility and some kindness" and where Mr. Watson, one of the British leaders, held American Methodism and ordination and the *Christian Guardian* in "sneering contempt." He did all that he could to warn the Canadian conference against union. One wing of Canadians, however, and prime among them his brothers, increasingly saw a union with British Wesleyans as the only feasible answer to their problems and their situation. With an alliance worked out and a British Wesleyan as leader of the Canadian conference they hoped that they would finally have the overseas support that they needed for their work, both internal and missionary. Hopefully they could also, once and for all, prove their essential loyalty and political good faith by working with the British Wesleyans.

From England, George Ryerson warned them by every letter

against the union. He increasingly wrote of his disillusion with politics which he saw as a "mystery of iniquity" and with the intensely political aspect of the cause he had come to champion: "Don't lean upon an arm of flesh, I mean an arm of flesh in the most specious and seductive form—human opinions. You are scarcely aware of how much of our religion stands upon no other basis. The Papists amidst much rubbish have retained the whole truth; Protestants have horribly marred it in their fear of retaining any of its rust."[8]

George was powerfully attracted to the otherworldliness of the popular young English preacher, Edward Irving, and to what he considered a true Christian holiness and purity in the sect which was gathering around Irving. By March, 1833, when Egerton arrived in England as a new Canadian emissary for negotiation, George had withdrawn from the Methodist cause entirely.

Thirty years old, recently bereaved, backwoods preacher, journalist and controversialist-pamphleteer, Egerton Ryerson landed in Portsmouth. In a twenty-day voyage, he "was sick for fourteen days, ate nothing, thought little, and enjoyed nothing. . . . Thanks be to the God of heaven, earth and sea for His protection, blessing and prosperity."

The psychological-sociological jargon of our time has never devised a phrase more vividly descriptive than "culture shock." Generations of colonial exiles went back to England as to home. They called it "over home" when they planned to go and many of them, their children and their children's children, still called it "over home" when they would never go. "It is very important that you should go home," John Ryerson wrote to Egerton, discussing the proposed mission. "You will endeavour, in every way you can, to convince the British Conference of the manifest injustice and wickedness of sending missionaries to this country." To Egerton Ryerson, as to his brothers, England was home in that her culture, her institutions and customs were the parent ones. But they were by no means all to be accepted holus-bolus by her enlightened children. There was in this, as in all other family relationships, the rejection by the young of what seemed to them outmoded or mistaken in the old.

Furthermore one catches in the words of the brothers a very real feeling of the newness, the second chance, the freshness of their world —not an Eden, never that to these stern preachers of man's sins, but in some senses a Canaan. Theirs was the responsibility and the opportunity to work in a new world with a sense of a second chance, a fresh start, and perhaps to avoid some of the ancient errors. So it seemed to

George as he wrote of the cholera from London: "The judgments of God are spreading apace—the Cholera is more deadly in London, and it has now broken out in Ireland and in the citie of Paris where it is said to be very destructive. You need no other evidence of its being a work of God than to be informed that it is made the public mock of the infidel population of this city. . . . I am sorry to see that you have copied some of this blasphemy into your paper. Do not do so any more until you are better informed lest you be found fighting against God."[9]

In England Egerton travelled and preached to Methodist congregations, carrying on negotiations for union with the Wesleyans as he went. In his church functions he had long since established both competence and confidence. He obviously saw this move as almost certainly a necessity for Canadian Methodism and, hopefully, as equally an opportunity for its strengthening. Underneath the laconic words of his journal reports, an adventuring excitement moved him too, as he first experienced the easy flowing together of past and present that is England's special quality and felt himself in real contact with Methodism's history. On the first Sunday morning in London, he did not follow much of the sermon: "I could not pretend to offer any opinion, as my mind was too much excited, and my feelings at times quite overcome." A few days later, quite recovered in equanimity but deeply impressed, he was guest speaker at a mid-week service in John Wesley's Chapel, the very heart of Methodism: "This evening I preached my first sermon in England, in City Road Chapel. . . . This is called Mr. Wesley's Chapel, having been built by him. . . . Alongside is Mr. Wesley's dwelling-house, and in the rear of it rest his bones. . . . In front of this chapel, on the opposite side of the street, are the celebrated Bunhill Fields burying ground, among whose memorable dead rests the dust of the venerable Isaac Watts, John Wesley's mother, John Bunyan, Daniel Defoe . . . ."[10]

The union with British Wesleyans, successful in its negotiation but unfortunate in its Canadian outcome of several years of unease and dissension, was only the first and official reason for Ryerson's trip. He served two other functions while in England, soliciting all over the country for funds for the new Academy at Cobourg and presenting at the Colonial Office Canadian petitions regarding the Church-Education-Clergy Reserve question. Here he was teamed with William Lyon Mackenzie who had been in England for over a year, since he and the *Advocate's* office had been attacked by a gang of young Compact-partisans in 1832. Mackenzie and Ryerson were incongruous companions, both physically and temperamentally. Ryerson was praised by British Wesleyans for "the urbanity of his manners" and "his pious deportment." Mackenzie, neither urbane nor conventionally pious, was a constant storm of energy and emotional intensity. But the two shared the most important thing, a committed antagonism to Church Establishment and all its supporters in Canada. Moreover, each had intellectual, temperamental and professional capacities which the other could and did respect and appreciate. So, just now in London, they were allies and close co-workers.

Only by direct petition could a man or a group be heard outside of the regular government channels. The process was standard; it presented no strangeness to Colonial Office officialdom or to a practised agitator-petitioner like Mackenzie. To this role Ryerson, however, was a stranger, but as always, under any intellectual stimulus, he was quick both to learn and to assimilate experience to practical ends. Though he wrote of impatience at the delay in his return to Canada, he was both challenged and excited by his function as an explicator of the Canadian situation.

Before Mackenzie sailed for Canada in June, he and Ryerson talked to Joseph Hume who was actively partisan for the Canadian reformers in the British Parliament. Ryerson also had interviews regarding the Clergy Reserves question with both Mr. Ellice and Mr. Stanley, then Under-Secretary and Secretary for Colonial Affairs. After Mackenzie left, he was the Canadian representative for the side of the Dissenting Clergy; at the same time, Christopher Hagerman was presenting the case of the Anglican Church:

I have had two interviews with Mr. Secretary Stanley on the subject of the Address, and have drawn up a statement of the grounds on which the House of Assembly, and great body of the people of Upper Canada, resist the pretensions and claims of the Episcopal Clergy.[11]

I have been two nights to the House of Commons; heard them debate one night on Slavery in the West Indies & the other on tithes in Ireland ... there was not much *dignity* in the collected wisdom of the nation in some of the proceedings. I went into the Court of King's Bench & heard Chief Justice deliver a charge to a jury on a civil case. ... I have visited several Public Institutions ... to examine the productions of human ingenuity, skill & superstition.[12]

He also visited the House of Lords, read the newspapers and sifted and analyzed what he found in them. Another stage in Ryerson's growing, maturing process was well underway: the pious clergyman who at home had learned to live so closely with the competent journalist watched people and events in England and came to his own conclusions relevant to his place and his people in Upper Canada.

Nothing in Ryerson's writing career is as remarkable as the series of "Impressions made by our late visit to England" which began to appear in the *Guardian* in October, 1833, shortly after his return to Canada. Their astuteness of analysis and the trenchant energy of their language are worlds removed from the dilettante jotting quality of more casual travellers' impressions.[13] The young man of thirty spoke his mind with all the effectiveness of a senior statesman of seventy. His words carry the weight of his own complete confidence and conviction. For Ryerson had seen, heard and made up his mind on certain important matters while on the spot in England; when he threw the power of his best rhetoric behind his decisions, he achieved a journalistic level that was very high indeed. He also brewed a storm of violent proportions in the inflammable air of Upper Canada. Of English Conservatives he wrote:

An English ultra tory is what we believe has usually been meant and understood in Canada by the unqualified term *tory*; that is, a lordling in power, a tyrant in politics, and a bigot in religion. In religion, he is superstitious or skeptical, as it happens; in morals, he is profane or devout, sensual or abstemious, spendthrift or miser, as inclination and interest may prompt; in opinions, he is as intolerant as he is illiberal. This description of partizans, we believe, is headed by the Duke of Cumberland, and is followed not "afar-off" by that powerful party, which presents such a formidable array of numbers, rank, wealth, talent, science, and literature, headed by the Hero of Waterloo. . . .[14]

Now and always, Ryerson's opinions were formed, stretched, and modified by personal and ideological imperatives which at once pushed him towards order, stability and tradition and pulled him to independence and freedom. Both the reality and the dreams of the men he came from and the men he knew were rooted in the land. The best and the only development for Canada that he could envision was a solidly land-based society of God-and-property-respectful-men. Now and later his tradition and his temper of mind seemed to be closest to the English Whigs as he saw and described them in 1833:

The Whig appears to differ in *theory* from the tory in this, that he interprets the constitution, obedience to it, and all measures in regard to its administration, upon the *principles of expedience,* and is therefore always pliant in his professions, and is ever ready to suit his

measures to the *times*; an indefinite term, that also designates the most
extensively circulated daily paper in England, or in the world, which
is the leading organ of the whig party, backed by the formidable
power and lofty periods of the *Edinburgh Quarterly*: whereas the tory
maintains the implied contract of existing institutions and established
usages, and the authority of Revelation as the true foundation of
obedience to the civil government. To us, the theory of the truth lies
between the two; in practice there is but little difference. . . .[15]

Firm, decided, open, well-phrased, with the ironic bite always at
hand—this was fair measure for the two old-line parties. The Radicals
demanded sterner dealings—righteous invective and sarcasm:

The third political sect is called Radicals. . . . Mr. Attwood, the head
of the celebrated Birmingham political union, is (if we may judge
from hearing him speak two or three times in the House of Commons) a conceited, boisterous, hollow-headed declaimer. Never did we
hear any public man speak, of whom we formed so unfavourable an
opinion as of Thomas Attwood.
Radicalism in England appeared to us to be but another word for
Republicanism, with the name of King instead of President. This
school, however, includes all the Infidels, Unitarians, and Socinians
in the Kingdom; together with a majority of the population of the
manufacturing districts.[16]

The October 30 instalment of the "Impressions" finishes with a "To
be continued." Whatever may have been Ryerson's original further
impressions and intentions, he was never able to finish them as first
drafted. On the 30th, the very day of the "Impressions'" appearance,
Mackenzie printed a second edition of the *Advocate* to declare his
most violent brand of warfare on the *Guardian*: it "has gone over to
the enemy, press, types & all, & hoisted the colours of a cruel vindictive
tory priesthood." Ryerson had "struck a deadly blow" to the liberty of
Upper Canadians; he, Mackenzie, had been "the dupe of a jesuit in
the garb of a methodist preacher." For the first time, Ryerson was
smeared with the tar of a turncoat hypocrisy; neither in his lifetime
nor since has his reputation fully recovered from the taint.

The entire province seethed with factional politics and Methodists
were particularly edgy, distrustful of their brand new Union and of
the British preachers who had begun to arrive in Canada. William
Ryerson, feeling himself exiled to Kingston and at the mercy of a
newly-arrived, cocky young Irish minister named Hetherington, had
little patience or sympathy for Egerton at this time: "Through the
mercy of God we are all well at present and not quite starved or frozen

to death.... It is rather unfortunate that if you do not intend to flatter or conciliate the Tory party in this country at the expense of the feelings of many of your valuable Friends, you should express yourself in such a way as to be altogether misunderstood by both friends and foes in every part of the country...."[17]

Methodists attacked Ryerson as bitterly from within the church as Mackenzie and his supporters did from without. They were increasingly rubbed raw by the Union: here was the man who had negotiated it. Their pitch of feeling against the government set, "The Family Compact," was already high; now they could and did turn with fury on a leader who seemed to have bungled one cause and betrayed another. Brother John, whose energy of nature most consistently came through his pen into his eager, vivid words, communicates a chaos of disorder and dissent: "There is no union & no prospect of any, between the two congregations, so long as Mr. Hetherington remains there. The bitterness of his feelings beggers all description.... If the British conference will allow its members to throw firebrands, arrows & death around in this way & reprobate their proceedings after this manner with impunity, they are very different men from what I have always taken them to be. As weak and imperfect as we are, we would kill or cure a person who would proceed in this manner in short order."[18] A few weeks later, with terse finality John summed up the opinions of growing numbers of Canadian Methodists: "If this is the way we are to be governed & if this is the state of the connection at home, the Resolutions of *Union,* on parchment or paper, is a miserable farse."[19]

Reprimands and answers flew back and forth between Ryerson and various ministers of the conference and at the same time, Mackenzie's continuing attacks had to be repudiated in the *Guardian*. Methodists had been very clever at using, exploiting and disciplining this young man's abilities; now he had gone too far for many of them. Greatly to the credit of all concerned, however, as he defended his position week after week, his arguments gradually persuaded the people that he was reclaimable. To one protesting group of colleagues Ryerson replied: "If our Conference will place a watchman upon the wall of our Zion, and then allow its members to plunge their swords into his bowels whenever they think he has departed from his duty, without even giving him a court-martial trial, then they are a different description of men from what I think they are. If, as you say, I have been guilty of imprudent conduct, or even 'misrepresented my brethren,' make your complaint to my Presiding Elder, according to discipline, and then may the decision of the Committee be published in the *Guardian,* or anywhere else that they may say."[20]

Amongst all the outcry, the dismayed speculation of his colleague, James Evans, as to Ryerson's possible motivation does, in fact, come closest to the truth: "I can only account for your strange, and I am sure, un-Ryersonian conduct and advice on one principle—that there is something ahead which you, through your superior political spy glass, have discovered and thus shape your course, while we land-lubbers, short-sighted as we are, have not even heard of it."[21]

Ryerson did foresee trouble in the Radicals' path; he did wish to warn simple ignorant people against being swept towards violent, treasonable revolt. And his fears were strengthened, his own opinions buttressed and his reading of a minister's and an editor's responsibilities to the people underlined, by the violence growing in the temper of the people. On one such occasion an angry Kingston mob burned Mackenzie and himself in effigy; outbreaks like this one dismayed him—they were symptoms of a wild energy which could only, ultimately, destroy.

He could not possibly have been heroically, independently reckless of consequences. By nature, by conviction, and by training he was quite unlikely to fall into any heroic stance, because he, and Methodism, made very sharp distinctions between man and God, men and heroes. Likewise, he, and Methodism, assessed very realistically the powers and pressures affecting men. Methodism moulded men to act with an independence of conscience voluntarily limited, within a framework of corporately determined "law." As within the Discipline and the Conference, so within the state: a man's responsibility was to push where his conscience dictated pushing, but also *not* to push to the breaking point the order which sustained him.

Furthermore, Ryerson's experience of England had confirmed all this in him. If he saw the abounding evidences of "dark satanic mills" he does not record them, nor did they make any impression on him comparable to the picture of order, dignity, decorum, stability and power that he expected, desired, and therefore found. He was young, colonial, provincial, and, compared to Mackenzie for instance, warmly illusioned about England, impressed by being there at all and more impressed by the sense of having a certain place and a certain dignity in the transpiring of momentous events. Naturally he relished the courtesy with which he was treated by men like Mr. Stanley and the Methodist leaders; naturally as he watched the Commons and the Lords he admired a degree of knowledgeability and urbanity still woefully lacking on the Upper Canadian Legislative scene. And certainly he sensed and was awed by the immense resources of power, both intellectual and physical, that underpinned the government of Britain and that could be turned against any colony that spun out of its appointed orbit.

On November 8, in the early days of all the outcry, Ryerson married again. Mary Armstrong was, he says, the "eldest daughter of a pious and wealthy merchant," James Armstrong, of York. Some of his letters from England suggest by their tone of impatience to get home, that Mary had agreed to marry him on his return. At any rate he and his children, John and Lucilla, now had a family setting again. If Mary was chosen more for the qualities which then reminded her husband of Hannah than for her own, she gained at least the considerable satisfaction of a solid home establishment. She had also to accustom herself to, and perhaps to enjoy, the position attendant upon the wife of a public, and just now a notorious, Upper Canadian.

Chapter 6

The Rebellion Years

Between 1825 and 1834 Ryerson learned and developed to competence, sometimes to brilliance, the skills upon which he effectively drew in his later life and career. These years were, career-wise, his formative ones, and in them he progressed uncharted miles from the callow and anxious young man who had ridden off on his first circuit to preach to the Upper Canadian Israel. The slightly gaunt and fanatic-eyed young man of an early engraving had now been transformed into the confident, competent, eminently presentable young man of the Andrew Gush portrait. He had lost nothing of purpose, dedication or zeal in the change, but he had gained poise from a presence which he could count on to command respect and attention, and from the consciousness of tests and challenges undertaken and overtaken, of difficult missions accomplished. Egerton Ryerson was now the best suited of all the Canadian Methodists for the undertaking of their ambassadorial missions.

The only real uniqueness of Methodism among fundamentalist churches was its organizational stress. This was its greatest strength and its greatest appeal to a pioneer population: unsure of your status politically, quakingly unsure of your state of grace, you could find some purpose and security and ample motivation towards a life of good works within the organization of Methodism. From Wesley's eighteenth-century sense of pattern and purpose, from his early insistence on ties with the organized hierarchy of Anglicanism, from his devising of rules of order, a Discipline to contain and support his people, to the Upper Canada conference which in the early years deployed Ryerson's forces to such good effect, demonstrates one among many successful practical applications of Methodism's development.

Apprenticed as preacher and teacher-missionary, journeyman-journalist and emissary, Ryerson was now a master-Guildsman. Now, in maturity, he was not entirely malleable to his seniors and elders as "the Boy Preacher" had been, for his own development continued both within and without the bounds of Methodism. At thirty Ryerson rested more easily with his own ambitions than he had at twenty; his diary entries contain fewer of the soul-searchings that in the early years ranged from the agonized to the self-conscious and sentimental. His oppressive, compulsive sense of "unworthiness" had gradually given over to a healthy enjoyment of his own intellectual powers and a sensible enjoyment of the healthy physique that made their use and development possible.

The doctrinaire unworldliness, requisite and becoming in the young convert, had far less place in the mature man. Now, his consciousness of both duty and opportunity to serve the interests of his wife and children and to function as a leader in his time and place, rested in sometimes precarious balance with his consciousness of duty to God. Ryerson never did submerge the "thirsting after the honours of this world" that had seemed to him in his early twenties a deplorable weakness; a powerful mind and a healthy ego pushed him on. He increasingly allowed himself more satisfaction from the exercise of his gifts and skill and, succeeding in their use, he grew in confidence of his own powers as a leader. Besides he could, of course, in his time and calling, and he *did*, sincerely consider all his work to be for the good of the people and to the ultimate glory of God.

Upper Canada, too, grew up around him. York jumped from a little garrison town of one thousand in 1825, to a city of ten thousand, incorporated as Toronto in 1834. Its claim to city-status in any cosmopolitan sense was tenuous indeed. It was *still* a frontier town of mud and rampant epidemics, a tight little society whose pretensions were both pathetic and ludicrous, but always understandable in terms of its isolation, its need for status and its rapidly expanding citizenry, whose swift growth in numbers constantly taxed to its very bounds its own corporate ability to function adequately. Other towns and villages were growing just as rapidly as York, some, in proportion to their size and history, more so: in the space of a few years, months even, a promising village could thrive where only a likely millsite or a crossroads had been. The frontier of the backwoods had been pushed back, concession by concession, and though there were many thousands of emigrants arriving yearly who would be challenged to succeed or fail by the virgin forest, there were many others who had survived and achieved the first clearing, settling stages.

A number of the people whom Ryerson had preached to on his first circuits had moved from the log cabins where they had been glad to entertain the preacher, to neat frame houses; all the rest worked, crop by crop, to do the same. The conditions of the land, its life and its people were still stubbornly rough, crude and hard. For all that, however, patterns of civic and social order had taken shape and were beginning to spread their networks over the country, with the surveyed roads and the trails, still notoriously atrocious mud-bogs though they often were, their arteries. Somewhere in the future, just barely discernible, lay the land as it would be, never in the soft ordered parishes of John Strachan's dream, no smoothly curving Ararat, but still, tamed and ordered to its own requirements, to Ryerson and to many others a reasonably "sunny part of America" on its own terms.

All capacities for the civilizing of the province were constantly strained to their utmost, inevitably by reason of its rapid growth in population, the factional wrangling in its government, and the delay and liability to error in its communications with the Colonial Office in London. As the people slowly grew in security and confidence, however, they were able to think somewhat beyond the next day's, the next season's, the next year's bare subsistence, to their own and their children's future comfort. Now, the thoughts of all who were themselves literate, and of many who were not, could move sometimes beyond the heated political present to a future where schooling for their children would give them resources for advancement that the land alone, though precious, could not offer them.

Ryerson did indeed look through a "political spyglass" with astute appraisal, but he was neither unique in that nor demonstrably "right" while others were "wrong." The particular and lasting quality of his maturity was, rather, a combination of practical vision, ambition and dogged determination, all of them together directed unremittingly on the ordering and civilizing of Upper Canada into a corporate community, religiously by the private exercise of each man's conscience, and socially by the public education of all the children. By 1834, by reason of his family's past and its choice of Upper Canada, through his experience of the province and its people and, lately, through his observations of Britain which pointed up real differences to the cancellation of sentimental similarities, Ryerson felt Canadian. This sense of identity and the responsibility attendant on it could and did sometimes outvote Methodism. And both, in the mature man who assessed his own physical and intellectual capacities and then pushed them to the limit, could be severely jostled by ambition.

"I value what I hold to be the cardinal doctrines, and morals and interests of Christianity, above either Churchism or Methodism. . . . I do not understand the hairsplitting casuistry which separates the man from the Christian."[1] Ryerson's cornerstone personal creed had to accommodate this conviction with doing whatever he saw to be done, to insure that "the land of my birth and affections is made prosperous and happy."[2] And there *was* also the prideful element that added both strength and vulnerability to his complexity of talents, sketched with true Methodist "every brother's keeper" frankness by Dr. Richey, a colleague: "I do not flatter you in saying, that on no man in Upper Canada does the peace of our Church and of the Province so much depend, as on yourself. May all your powers be employed for good! Guard against the fascination of political fame. It will do no more for you on a dying bed than it did for Cardinal Wolsey. O! that your fine mind were fully concentrated upon the community of Heaven."[3]

Six-year old John Ryerson died in September, 1835, probably of the dysentery commonly called "summer complaint", then the cause of so many children's death: "He became a perfect skeleton, yet continued to walk until within ten minutes before his death. After attempting to take a spoonful of milk, he leaned back his head and expired in my arms, without the slightest visible struggle. . . . O my dear Brother, I feel as a broken vessel in this bereavement of the subject of so many anxious cares and fond hopes."[4]

In November, 1835, Mary and Egerton sailed for England, once again on a three-purpose mission. Officially, he was to petition for a charter and government grant for the Academy at Cobourg and to solicit funds from private individuals, since it was already in desperate financial straits. William Lord, the chairman of its Board, leaves no doubt as to the situation's urgency—"*Beg, beg, beg* it all. It must be done! *You must stay in England until the money is got.* Use every effort, harden your face to flint, and give eloquence to your tongue. This is your calling. Excel in it! Be not discouraged with a dozen of refusals in succession. The money must be had, and it must be begged. My dear Brother, work for your life. . . ."[5]

Unofficially, but just as importantly, Ryerson expected to do what mending he could between the British Wesleyans' parent conference and the Canadian Methodists. In principle their Union had seemed

to him to be an eminently reasonable, expedient solution of juris-
dictional problems between two sister churches. In practice, in the
hands of all too fallible men, it had turned out to be at best an armed
truce, more usually a pitched battle between the British and the Canadian preachers and their factions. And then, always at his back he felt
the power and pressure of the Canadian wing of the Established
Church, epitomized for him by John Strachan and the official
Anglican attitude towards the Clergy Reserves. Ryerson thoroughly
relished the sense of power to move events; he had every intention of
presenting his arguments for the cause of justice, as he saw it, wherever he could put a foot in the door. As events turned out, there was
chance and more than time enough to do so. The Ryersons did not
return to Canada until June of '37, well after the birth of their
daughter Sophia, the first child of Egerton's second marriage and the
person who grew up to be closer to her father than anyone else in his
entire life.

The Academy's charter was granted as desired, even with the words
"Wesleyan Methodist *Church*" approved in it when Ryerson pressed
for them, though such a body was unknown in law in England at that
time. The problem of funds was harder: no direct grant was made
from the British government, the Legislative Council of Upper
Canada obstructed a bill passed by the Legislature for support to the
sum of sixteen thousand dollars, and Sir Francis Bond Head delayed
funds, even when instructed directly by Lord Glenelg, the Colonial
Secretary, to give some. Throughout all negotiations in England, however, Ryerson himself was treated with respect. He enjoyed the role
of informed advisor and he did not doubt that he had pleaded well,
in the best interests of both his church and his homeland:

I was applied to, and did, in my individual capacity, communicate to
the Colonial Secretary Lord Glenelg and Under-Secretary James
Stephen frequently, and in one or two instances at great length, on the
posture of Canadian affairs; and the parties and principal questions
which have divided and agitated the Canadian public. I repeatedly
received the thanks of the Secretary of State for the Colonies, for the
pains I had taken in these matters. . . .

In fact, in the course of this mission his self-confidence moved well
over into complacency: "I think I have good reason to believe that
much more correct and decided views are entertained by His Majesty's
ministers and many public men in England, in respect to the interests
and government of the Canadas, than were possessed by them six
months ago."[6]

He also busied himself in writing a series of eight letters for the *Times,* printed there between June, 1836, and January, 1837. The first six were from "A Canadian," to Joseph Hume and John Arthur Roebuck, as the two reformers most concerned with agitation for insurrection in the Canadas. The last two were addressed to the Secretary of State for the Colonies. In these, as if convinced by detachment from the heated Canadian scene and supported by his residence on British soil, Ryerson assured the British public of the loyalty of most Canadians. He divorced himself completely from the cause of reform as defined and practised by Mackenzie and the Radicals, and, by implication and advice, he divorced all loyal Canadians from the Radical cause as well.

The letters were effective enough in their function in Britain. But bound into a pamphlet and circulated in Canada in the tense months preceding the rebellion, they created another furious storm. He was called "devious," "cunning," a "turncoat hypocrite." The name of Ryerson became anathema to every reformer. Mackenzie's most violent supporters threatened to "hang him from the first tree they came to" if they caught him; in the tensions of the Rebellion's worst days, they may well have meant their threat. Certainly his friends and brothers thought that he was in actual physical danger.

However, even wild threats of violence were borne more easily than the abuse of former friends and colleagues. One wing of the Methodists, finding union with the British Wesleyans absolutely intolerable, had broken away into the Methodist Episcopal Church. The men who separated, and many of those who stayed, blamed Ryerson for the Union in the first place. They felt that he had indeed sold them out to the British—religion and politics so firmly glued together, were they not, as Mackenzie trumpeted, totally betrayed by this man? In November of 1837, Anson Green, a friendly colleague, wrote to him: "I pity you most sincerely. You have a storm about your ears that you must bear if you do not bow before it. In these perilous times a man scarcely knows what to advise. I fear that destruction waits us on either hand. With the Radicals we are Tories; and with the Tories we are Rebels."[7]

No moment of glamour or glory attaches to Ryerson's name during the few intense days of Rebellion excitement or during the gloomy, unsettled, dismayed months that followed. The Ryersons had returned from England in June of '37 and had been posted to the Kingston Church. In early December Egerton travelled as far as Cobourg on his way to Toronto. He had planned to go on to visit his parents in

Norfolk county, but he stayed in Cobourg on the advice of friends and because of a letter from his brother William in Toronto: "Brother John thinks it will not be wise for you to come through all the way from Kingston. You would not be safe in visiting this wretched part of the country at the present. You know the feelings that are entertained against you."[8]

He missed all of the crisis' excitement in Toronto, the wild rumour, the odd spectacle in the St. Lawrence marketplace of "a large number of persons serving out arms to others as fast as they possibly could,"[9] the strange assortment of men and weapons who marched up Yonge Street to meet the rebels, and the disordered anti-climax of the encounter at Montgomery's Tavern. William Ryerson marched with the loyal defenders of Toronto and reported to his brother: "After a little skirmishing in which we had three men wounded but none killed, the main body commenced a very spirited attack on their headquarter's at Montgomery's large house. After a few shots from two six-pounders, and a few volleys of musketry, the most of the party fled and made their escape. The rest of them were taken prisoners. There were also three or four killed and several wounded. After which His Excellency ordered the buildings to be burnt to the ground and the whole force returned to the city. All the leaders succeeded in making their escape."[10]

Egerton Ryerson was not there to participate in the pitiful human aftermath when the Toronto jail was crowded with the arrested men, most of them ignorant settlers who only dimly grasped the issues for which they had taken up arms against the Queen and who only now realized that their offence was treason, its penalty death. Egerton Ryerson was not present to take an active part in petitioning for the pardon of Lount and Matthews, though he did write a strong letter to Sir George Arthur, counselling against their execution. Their sentences were unwarranted for a political offence, he said, and savagely punitive rather than just. John Ryerson wrote him of following the two men to their execution:

Very few persons present except the military & the ruff scruff of the city. The general feeling is in total opposition to the execution of these men. At their execution they manifested *very good* composure. Sheriff Jarvis burst into tears when he entered the room to prepare them for execution. . . . They ascended the scaffold & knelt down on the *drop,* the rope was fastened to their necks while they were on their knees. Mr. Richardson engaged in prayer & when he came to that part of the Lord's Prayer, *Forgive us our trespasses as we forgive them that trespass against us,* the drop fell.[11]

Brother William wrote of the disintegration of public morale in York and of the panic emigration to the States that many planned:

...Dissatisfaction with the state of things is, I fear, increasing from day to day. Emigration to the States is the fear of the hour. It is indeed going on to an extent truly alarming and astonishing. A deputation has been sent from this city to Washington to negotiate with the American government for a tract of land on which to form a settlement or colony. They have returned, and say that they met with a most gracious reception, encouragement and success beyond their most sanguine expectations. An emigration society has been formed embracing some of the leading citizens. Its object is to commence a colony in the Iowa Territory, on the Mississippi River. A very large class are becoming uneasy, and many of the best inhabitants of the country, as to industry and enterprise, are preparing to leave. My own spirit is almost broken down. I feel, I assure you, like leaving Canada too, and I am not alone in those feelings; some of our friends whom you would not suspect, often feel quite as much down in the throat as I do.[12]

This was the colony's lowest ebb. Militant reformers, defeated and disgraced, were engaged in a futile, last-ditch stand on Navy Island, captured, sentenced, or penned up in Toronto awaiting trial. Or, temporarily escaped, they were still and, hopefully, invisible. But the militant were a very small minority; for every one of them there were a hundred men and women who felt afraid and defeated in spirit. Disaster had cut away all confidence, both in their present rights and in the possibility of achieving future freedom by any means whatsoever.

Egerton Ryerson's function in these months does not signal to us across time with any flamboyance of appeal whatever; no one gesture or decisive act of will makes an emotional bond with us. Mackenzie nervously rallies his ridiculously inept troops, Fitzgibbon and Bond Head gallop up Yonge Street to head off the attackers, Lount and Matthews walk to the gallows "with entire composure and firmness of step," John Strachan indefatigably visits the prisoners and preaches in the jail—and Egerton Ryerson sits in his Kingston parsonage and *writes*.

Ineradicably, there clings around the passivity and the colourlessness of his role in the actual Rebellion days an aura of mean-spiritedness. But in the following five years, through the confusions of the Rebellion's aftermath, Ryerson's contributions to the present and the future of a colony so badly shattered in reputation and self-esteem were again to be of prime importance. His brothers and others pressured him to reassume the editorship of the *Guardian:* "It is a great blessing that Mackenzie and radicalism are down, but we are in imminent danger of being brought under the domination of a military and high-church oligarchy, which would be equally bad, if not infinitely worse. Under the blessing of Providence, there is one remedy and only one; and that is, for you to take the editorship of the *Guardian* again."[13]

Protesting both unfitness and unwillingness, Egerton still agreed to do whatever Conference wished. His colleagues drafted his editorial services in June of 1838. Once again responsible for Canadian Methodism's official voice in the press, yet determined on his own rights in free speech, he stated his editorial policy. That of course, had first of all to do with Upper Canada's still bubbling witches' brew, the Clergy Reserves, then with a provincial system of education, his own growing preoccupation and the coming recipient, he hoped, of the revenue from the Reserves. He made an effort to instruct his still naïve and avidly partisan readers on his journalistic policy. Though all Methodists together, he insisted that his printed opinions were not necessarily theirs: "To be the mere scribe of the opinions of others, and not to write what we think ourselves, is a greater degradation of intellectual and moral character than slavery itself. . . . In doctrines and opinions we write what we believe to be the truth, leaving to others the exercise of a judgment equally unbiased and free."[14]

And, most important of all, as he reassumed leadership, he firmly stated that the field of education was his public goal. It was also to be the dominant ambition of his next forty years: "In nothing is this Province so defective as in the requisite available provisions for, and an efficient system of, general education. Let the distinctive character of that system be the union of public and private effort. . . . To Government influence will be spontaneously added the various and combined religious influence in the country in the noble, statesmanlike, and divine work of raising up an elevated, intelligent, and moral population."[15]

Chapter 7

The Waiting Game

Egerton Ryerson became the strong man of Upper Canadian education in 1844 when he was appointed its Assistant Superintendent, under the nominal headship of Robert Jameson, the province's Vice-Chancellor. The years between 1838, when under post-Rebellion pressures and fears he took over the *Guardian* again, and 1842, when he became Principal of Victoria College, the former Upper Canada Academy, at Cobourg, were far less years of growth than of endurance.

Politically, he and his *Guardian* policies were under attack at all times, from without and from within his own church. Each faction of the press waged constant bitter, carping, suspicious war against the other; all segments of the public joined in an enthusiastic revival of free speech on public questions, inaugurated by the "Durham meetings" of 1839 held all over the province, to argue, oppose and support the reforms that Lord Durham suggested. Factionalism, among all the Protestant churches of the province, was rampant. Methodism, in its and in Upper Canada's early days, had served a very definite function in giving order and cohesion to the lives of many individuals, bringing them together into groups which, while basically religious, also had social coherence. Now, in the inevitable process of growth and change, its society-ordering function was becoming quite lost in the shattering and fragmenting of its internal factionalism.

Ryerson never wrote better than when he felt the ground on which he stood in dire danger and himself personally challenged by John Strachan, his old adversary. Elevated from Archdeacon to Bishop of Toronto, Strachan was now able to command more influence in the Established Church's total hierarchy on both sides of the Atlantic. His enduring effort was to ensure against constitutional reform jeopardizing any part of his church's traditional rights and responsibilities. He

82

had not moved an inch from his old position, that *all* of the proceeds of the Clergy Reserves should go to the Establishment, that any compromise whatever trampled "on the faith of the British Government by destroying the birthright of all the members of the Established Church who are now in the province, or who may hereafter come into it; it promotes error, schism and dissent, and seeks to degrade the clergy of the Church of England to an equality with unauthorized teachers. . . ."[1]

A compromise Bill on the Reserve lands was proposed in 1840, suggesting that one half of the proceeds of sale of the remaining lands should go to the Anglican and Presbyterian churches, and the other half to "other religious bodies desiring to share in it," the funds "for the support of religious instruction within the province." Neither Ryerson nor Strachan was pleased, but, characteristically, Ryerson accepted what he saw as inevitable: "Up to the present time I have employed my best efforts, by every kind of argument, persuasion and entreaty, to get the proceeds applied simply and solely to educational purposes. . . . This is unattainable, and is rendered so by an original provision of our Constitution (of 1791), as stated by the Governor."[2]

Both Ryerson's strength and his vulnerability to attack always lay in his willingness to see necessity and to adapt to it, particularly when he was persuaded that a constitutional, legal principle was involved. He stopped short of tampering with the structure he found essential for Canada's health and growth. But Strachan had always moved as if he, personally, were built into the structure, as indeed in first principles he felt his church to be. He had always fought from that position of strength and now no compromise was good enough. As the Bill was pushed towards its passing, he spoke with maddening, condescending foreknowledge, secure and, in fact, later justified in his confidence of the Bishops' support "at home": "At the same time I have no fear of its ever becoming law. But it may be useful, for its monstrous and unprincipled provisions will teach the Imperial Government the folly of permitting a Colonial Legislature to tamper with these great and holy principles of the Constitution, on the preservation of which the prosperity and happiness of the British Empire must ever depend."[3] After such majestic loftiness of certainty, only silence or sarcasm was possible. Ryerson chose, of course, to talk back to "John Toronto," as he derisively called Strachan: "After penning such an effusion, the Bishop might well betake himself to the Litany of his church, and pray to the good Lord to deliver him—from all blindness of heart; from pride, vain glory and hypocrisy; from envy, hatred and malice, and all uncharitableness."[4]

The hundreds of thousands of words that Ryerson directed against the Establishment as he saw it personified in John Strachan form the largest single Canadian mass of "defensive rhetoric." Later, when George Brown of the *Globe* thundered daily at "the Pope of Methodism," as he called Ryerson, the latter could and did answer back from even ground. But Ryerson in opposition to Strachan always felt himself beleaguered—as indeed he was; the Methodists were and always had been in the weak position. To Strachan and Canadian Anglicans, Methodism entailed far more adverse discrimination than the Methodists and particularly Ryerson himself, in his various missions overseas and now in his dealings with Lord Sydenham and then Lord Metcalfe, had encountered in officialdom in Britain.

To be of Strachan's church was to know your place, in Canada as in England, warmly supported and strongly a support in the great system which seemed certainly to embrace all in its chain of being, stretching unbroken from man through the crown to God. The Presbyterian church, though torn by factionalism, gave a security to its members too. They were, after all, members of a church which had fought through and won its place as Scotland's "Established." By its doctrine, by their experience and by their traditions, they were also both proud and tough—a Scotsman seemed to be born as fully clothed with his own identity as he was both individualized and clan-identified by his name. His mind, tempered by Calvinism, "was one of the toughest the world has ever had to deal with" and if, as Perry Miller has written, it is "impossible to conceive of a disillusioned Puritan," it is just as impossible to think of a disillusioned Scot. "No matter what misfortune befell him, no matter how often or how tragically his fellowmen failed him, he would have been prepared for the worst and would have expected no better."[5]

Ryerson, however, is a type of all the Methodists of his time. In him, his attitude and the positions he felt forced to take, there is written large a defensiveness, a negative identity only, that is certainly a part of Canada's social past, with its outcroppings just as surely in Canada's present. Still, in 1840, however worthy a man and strong an adversary he might be, Ryerson and his family were socially invisible to Strachan. It is strange to read that these two, who had already been titans in controversy for fifteen years, did not actually meet or talk to each other until 1842, when they were returning by the same stage from Kingston to Toronto: "For the first time in my life, I found

ROBERT HARRIS

A MEETING OF THE SCHOOL TRUSTEES

myself in company with the Lord Bishop of Toronto, and my legs locked in with his Lordship's. . . . It would be unpardonable to make remarks of a painful character upon one's neighbours, nor do I think it proper, generally speaking, to introduce them into travelling notes in any form; but there has been something so peculiar in the relations of 'John Toronto' and 'Egerton Ryerson' that I must beg in this case to depart from a general rule."

The Bishop advised Ryerson most affably on several matters—on scarcely any of which "did I see reason to differ from the Bishop"; when they finished their day of forced intimacy, Ryerson published his account as anecdote and homily in the *Guardian*, concluding with a suggestion that is both reasonable and laudable as policy, though neither in his day nor in ours often achieved: "How much asperity of feeling, and how much bitter controversy might be prevented, if those most concerned would converse privately with each other before they entered into the arena of public disputation."[6]

Ryerson's attitude goes beyond the social courtesy befitting Strachan as a public figure and a man who is fourteen years his senior, to a real pleasure, at age thirty-nine, in being recognized civilly by the Bishop and accorded the favour of his conversation. No matter what his competence in controversy, in spite of the considerable victories already won, he still felt as much a junior in clerical standing and social status as, rightly or wrongly, he imagined that Strachan thought him to be. Both men give tacit approval to social barriers by their attitudes; Ryerson and the Methodists, defensive and edgy, were too often apt to set the plain, honest man of God, the "homespun," in sharp contrast to the social civilized being, as if the two could not possibly live in one. And much that is strangely graceless in Ryerson's life and in Canada's comes from the long delayed reconciliation of the two.

Only once in his career, Ryerson came close to throwing up all his Canadian effort and moving to the States. In the spring of 1840, he had gone to the Conference in Baltimore, partly with a view to arranging a few months' stay, "to avail myself of some collegiate lectures, to pursue certain branches of science," certainly weary of his target position in the Canadian scene and probably making some soundings as to his possible reception into the American Methodist ranks. Nothing could have been more soothing: he found the Methodist connexion in advance of both the British and the Canadian and the people compatible—"the manners of the people in these Middle States are very like the manners of intelligent people in Upper Canada

—alike removed from the English haughtiness and Yankee coldness—simple, frank and unaffected."[7]

Most encouraging of all were the positions offered him: "I have the offer of one of the three or four largest Methodist Chapels in New York. I shall be appointed to one of the largest and most elegant in the city, where all the great meetings are held. . . ."[8] He was, as always, ambitious, restless to push forward to some new and rewarding challenge; he was also disillusioned by political and religious factionalism—and just now, temporarily, he was bone-weary of attack and of being attacked. "To interfere any more in civil contentions will be wasting the best part of my life to no purpose, for there seems to be no end to such things. To remain in Canada and be silent, will incur the hostility of both parties. . . . I would not return to the *Guardian* again for any earthly consideration."[9]

He came back to Toronto to find the Canada Conference in dire upheaval and himself under a violent crisis-attack. He stayed with the Canadian church, moved equally by the support and dependence of many colleagues and by his fighter's desire to clear his name and vindicate his policies. He and William Ryerson took a brief trip to England to attempt a last-minute reconciliation with the British conference. But all diplomacy failed. Though the resolutions based on their findings were passed on their return at a special Conference, one wing of Canada's Methodists withdrew from their Conference, badly weakening their ministry and throwing their membership into splinter-congregations.

Egerton spoke at the Conference for five hours, giving an entire listing and defence of his position with regard to the Union which he had negotiated in 1833. His climax was a moving Valedictory in the traditional confessional style of the Methodist class-meeting:

No young man in Canada had more friends amongst all Christian denominations than I had when the Union took place. Many of them have become my enemies. I can lose property without concern or much thought, but I cannot lose my friends and meet them in the character of enemies, without emotions not to be described. I feel that I have injured myself, and injured this Connexion, and I fear this province, not by my obstinacy, but by my concessions. This is my sin, and not the sins laid to my charge.[10]

His self-analysis was sound. His "concessions," for so every movement of conviction and diplomacy in politics and religion were interpreted by detractors whose stance may have been firmer than

Ryerson's, but whose vision was impaired, have shadowed his reputation through generations since.

Thomas Whitehead, the eighty-seven-year-old minister who chaired the Special Conference, was angry at all the "travelling gab" about Ryerson, as were all his supporters, clergy and people. There were many, however, eager and willing to prove that he was indeed, as Whitehead joked, "the sole cause of the rebellion in Heaven, by the fallen angels."[11]

Though he gave up his plans for moving to New York in 1840 and though the *Guardian* reported him appointed Principal of the Academy at Cobourg before his rushed trip to England with William, he did not take office there until 1842. In the years between, he ministered at the Adelaide Street church in Toronto and busied himself in ex-officio advice to and support of Lord Sydenham, in whose intentions for a truly Responsible Government he believed. Through this time Ryerson was more unsettled and uncertain than ever before in his life, and considerably wracked by ambition for public leadership. "Canada is indeed a plantation; & its inhabitants are a province of slaves," he wrote to an American colleague, Nathan Bangs, President of the Wesleyan University in Middletown, Connecticut. Some passages in the same letter suggest a serious consideration of politics:

Whether my continued silence in such circumstances is a virtue or a crime; or whether I should retire from the country, or remain & make one Christian, Open & decisive effort to secure for my fellow countrymen a free Constitution & equal rights amongst their Churches, is a perplexing question to me, as well as to my father-in-law & brothers. It is believed by some intelligent men who have talked on the subject, that if I would come out as the advocate of the country, there would be no doubt of success, from my knowledge of the subject, from a general, & as I think overweening confidence in my concentration, perseverance & energy & from the feelings of the country. It is also thought that if there should be a failure of success, I should then honorably retire to the U.S.[12]

In the midst of this personal uncertainty, and the frustration of feeling that he could preach, teach and write more effectively than circumstances allowed him to do, that his experience, drive and ambition qualified him for a level that was still not open to him and perhaps would never be, the Bill to incorporate Upper Canada Academy into Victoria College passed through Parliament and was finally ratified in the name of the Crown by Lord Sydenham. Early in September, 1841, its Board requested Ryerson to become Principal: "I need not say that our hope of success depends entirely upon raising the character of the College above that of Upper Canada Academy. To do this we must place at its head a person holding a commanding influence over that portion of society from whom we expect to receive support. . . .[13] The "support" necessary could manifest itself in public good will, but would be practically measured in dollars, and the willingness to send sons to the Academy to be educated. Ryerson accepted the post and the double challenge.

In October, 1841, at his solemn inauguration as Victoria's principal, Ryerson made his first policy speech on Education—his first statement of the main preoccupation of his next thirty-five years. He had certainly already thought of public service in education as a possible and desirable career. He had last talked to Lord Sydenham about such a possibility shortly before the latter's fall from his horse and subsequent death: "He intimated that he thought I might be more usefully employed for this country than in my present limited sphere; and whether there was not some position in which I could more advantageously serve the country at large . . . . I remarked . . . that I knew of no such position likely to be at the disposal of the Government except the Superintendent of Schools. . . ."[14]

His opening address's conventional modesty of tone is more than balanced by his own sense of his fitness. He had, in fact, leadership qualifications unique among Canadian Methodists in his time and all too rare in the ranks of administrators in ours: "My public life has been active rather than literary; and I can only account for the choice and solicitations of the Directors and friends of this Institution— and can only reconcile my own compliance with their requests— upon the principle laid down by the great Locke, that youth should be 'committed to the care of a virtuous and judicious Tutor, who is rather a man of experience in the world than of profound learning'. . . ."[15]

Once again, the Methodists were using Ryerson's talents well: once again he functioned to their needs. Their new College needed a strong Administrator-Principal — he gave them that with all his confidence and decision. He also brought to the policies he voiced, zest, a respect for learning, and a practical common sense which were going to be the hallmarks of his next thirty-five years. For Ryerson too was fortunate to be used so well and, in spite of intermittent strong feelings against him, to be valued so highly by his colleagues and peers. At thirty-eight he began a new career.

His opening address of October, 1841, and his formal Inaugural Address of June, 1842, together make a definitive statement of his educational aims, closely applicable to Victoria College as he then stated its aims, but broadly applicable to public education as he saw it then and continued to see it. He was first and always in this as in all else a pragmatic man, able to see the reality of a situation, to use it and to adapt to it—"education must be useful and suited to the intended pursuits of the educated." To be useful, it must be suited to the requirements of a particular people and society, it must be Christian "but not narrowly so," and it "must tend to form habits of industry." "Education is not a licence for idleness, but a means of active, honourable and useful enterprise."[16]

Ryerson sounded a perfect latter-day John Wesley as he outlined a practical education and counselled various exercises of self-improvement, chief among them early rising. The curriculum and discipline that he approved for Victoria have a dedicated rigour that is also reminiscent of Wesley's pedagogy, particularly as it was tried out in England at his Kingswood School. There was certainly to be no frippery or foolishness: girls and boys had previously gone to the Academy—but now, from the fall of 1842, only boys were admitted to the College; holidays gave rise to "serious evils"—therefore in the term of 1841 as in the previous year, there were no holidays except for Christmas and New Year's days. The Faculty had governing power over the students for seven days a week during term, and the responsibilities of all groups concerned with the life and management of the College were most clearly defined. He organized in general, Methodist, and in particular, Ryerson fashion, the system as he found it, to fit the principle in which he believed most firmly, that disciplined education was the path to self-improvement, to usefulness in society and to service of God.

Though conservative, dogmatic and unrelentingly authoritarian in administrative policies and practices, his inaugural address on "The Nature and Advantages of an English and Liberal Education" swung markedly towards a new-world, egalitarian liberalism of thought. Led to it by the practical concerns of the society he lived in, rather than through study of, or previous interest in educational theory, he spoke strongly and at length, for a balance towards an English language curriculum. His words contain a certain relish of defensive malice towards the classically oriented curriculum of tradition and John Strachan. "Much of the indifference to the study of the classics has doubtless originated in the extravagant estimate of them on the part of their professed admirers, who have, at the same time, affected a sovereign contempt—a contempt very generally the off-spring of ignorance—of the studies and beauties of the English Language."[17]

Once moved with his family to Cobourg, in 1842, Ryerson taught in the College as well as organizing and directing its administration and soliciting for its funds. He had taught briefly in his youth when he left home to be a Methodist; later he had assisted in the school for the Credit Indians; through his minister's career he had superintended and advised many young men. Best of all qualifications, he loved learning himself, simply as a process, a self-challenge and a private enjoyment. At Victoria, starting in one special position, as the Principal, he rapidly achieved another, as a teacher to be highly respected. His teaching, however, was not for triflers.

Former students reminisced about him with large measures of both admiration and awe, as one who "expected and exacted rather too much work from the average student. His own ready and affluent mind sympathized keenly with the apt, bright scholar . . . but he scarcely made sufficient allowance for the dullness or lack of previous preparation which failed to keep pace with him in his long and rapid strides; hence his censures were occasionally severe."[18] In August, 1842, he became a Doctor of Divinity of the Wesleyan University at Middletown. The respect of his friend, Nathan Bangs, and his American colleagues provided Ryerson with a title commensurate with his position at Victoria, one which he was pleased to adopt.

Meanwhile, political events in the newly-united Canadas churned restlessly, now and then violently, and Ryerson was not long content to look on from the outside. For a time a term in Canada seemed doom for its Governors: Lord Durham did not outlive his mission by many months, Lord Sydenham died in Canada in 1842, Sir Charles Bagot in 1843, and cancer had begun to kill Sir Charles Metcalfe before he took office. The burning question and test of these years was the interpretation and setting in motion of truly "responsible" government by both governors and people. Now, in 1844, a deadlock situation arose between Metcalfe and his Councillors, its origin the question of the limits of the Governor's power and of theirs, and its principle basic to the further development of Responsible Government.

Neither Ryerson's heart nor his ambitions lay dormant in Cobourg. He had lost none of the commitment or the sure knowledge of a certain power in his pen which he had developed in the years of

Guardian journalism and of negotiating missions overseas. In the thirties in certain crises, he had played a supportive role to constitutional officialdom; in the forties his position was, in his own eyes, that of a senior statesman and, on occasion, a personal adviser. In this capacity Lord Sydenham had accepted him with a healthy respect for his advice, his capacities and his powers to influence.

Moreover, Ryerson had certainly hoped to be appointed to the Superintendency of Schools that he and Lord Sydenham had talked of. His inaugural statements at Victoria show him invincibly confident as educational leader, a role that in his own mind he has already assumed. He had been both disappointed and offended when, under Governor Bagot, Mr. Murray was appointed Assistant Superintendent of Education under the nominal headship of Robert Jameson, the Provincial Secretary. But as it turned out Murray was treated as a clerk, "having no clerk himself, and having to submit his drafts of letters etc. to the Provincial Secretary."[19] Murray under Jameson meant the weak under the ruined, for Jameson was really an embarrassing hang-over from pre-Rebellion days, his function as a figurehead only just tolerated. Such a dependency as Murray's had no place at all in Ryerson's picture of the Superintendency.

Lord Metcalfe offered Ryerson the education post in the midst of the deadlock in the spring of 1844, with Baldwin and the Reform party violently opposed to his interpretation of Governor's role. John Ryerson, always the most gifted natural statesman of the brothers, saw and delineated Egerton's dilemma very clearly:

I am very well pleased with the idea of your being appointed to the office of Superintendent of Education—an office for which, I think, you are better qualified than any other person in the Province . . . You say the appointment is not political? . . . Yet, is it true, in point of fact, that the appointment is not political? . . . Would any one be continued in the office who did not support the Government for the time being? . . . Did not Lord Sydenham create this office for the very purpose of connecting the incumbent with the Government, and did he not have you in his mind's eye when he influenced this part of the enactment? . . . There is no doubt, however, that in case of the Baldwin Ministry again coming into power, the stool will be kicked from under you. And we should not forget that the success of the Governor-General, in carrying out his contemplated measures respecting the University, Colleges, etc., depends upon the Parliament . . . and what will be the result of another election, who can tell?[20]

Egerton made his choice; he deferred his immediate acceptance of the Superintendency to write a series of nine letters in defence of Lord Metcalfe. Amid the storm which then arose, honest shock at what seemed to be his blatant toadying for favour was as prominent as the vituperative abuses heaped on him by the Reform press, headed by the *Globe*. Whatever strength his conviction may have had in principle, his writing of the letters was politically astute—and, as events turned out, in his own favour. The Reform party was defeated in the October election, the government supported, and Egerton Ryerson then accepted the Education post knowing that, for some time at least, "the stool would *not* be kicked from under him."

When Ryerson threw the full force of pen and personality into public argument he adopted completely the role that came easily to him out of both Methodism and journalism: he *was* his every brother's keeper. He argued, not from opinion, but like a prophet, as if from the one and only truth. In principle devoted to freedom of thought and speech, his effect was, paradoxically, to strangle both in favour of his authority, which, sometimes by statement and sometimes by implication to him was clearly God-derived. There were many, both within and without his church, who never forgave Ryerson for this particular stand or for its success.

And in the midst of outcry and uproar, hardest for him to bear was the disillusion and antagonism of many Victoria students. For the time being, the prophet was *not* honoured in his own country. The warmly affectionate man beneath the mask of the law-giver really suffered under the students' resentful protests.

Chapter 8

Reading, Writing and Ryerson

Almost twenty years after he rode his first circuit as preacher, purveyor of books and learning, and organizer of all those who would listen and be led into Methodism, Egerton Ryerson became the organizer and administrator of Upper Canada's educational system. Far more of the land was settled; villages had grown into towns and muddy crossroads into villages. Toronto had been a city since 1834; now Kingston, for a time after Union in 1841 the legislative capital of the Canadas, felt a heady sense of prosperity and prestige. A dozen other towns, from Chatham to Cornwall, looked to a future where growth and progress were so inevitable that the words seemed synonymous. A generation of hard clearing and settling labour had marked its achievements on the country. Every year hundreds, perhaps thousands of acres were added to the total broken, harnessed, productive farmland of the province. Many of the "John Bushmen" of the 1820's had prospered beyond the first shanty, then log cabin stages of settling, and were now growing old in the stark neatness of Ontario brick farmhouses. All the rest worked and saved for that ineffable elevation in status and increase in security and confidence, when the greyed log houses which mellowed into the soil gave over to the spanking new brick or neat clapboard ones which dominated the land and signalled man's possession of it.

Vast as the cultivated acreage was now, in comparison to what it had been, the uncultivated tracts were still more vast. The possession of land and therefore of a stake in the future was always the chief impelling motive for the crowds of emigrants coming over far faster, now that steamships had begun to make a more predictably navigable highway of the Atlantic. Those who arrived with the most resources could afford to buy in settled or partially settled areas in the more developed lands "up front"; the rest had to try their fortunes on the poorer areas within the settled tracts or to test their strength and endurance, as the generations before them had done, in the backwoods bush. But there *was* more success to be seen everywhere, in the towns, in the farms and in the people.

Upper Canada had moved a little beyond a pioneer-subsistence society; consequently, everywhere, for the newcomer and for the veteran settler, there was some hope and security in the future beyond what a man's own mind, will and muscles could achieve. By the mid-forties, the province was a place where a man and his family could see and feel evidences of a growing social structure around them, reassuringly so in contrast to its precarious balance in the thirties. The time was right, finally, for a system of public education in Upper Canada, to replace all the well-meant and widely various experiments undertaken privately, contended for publicly, and legislated with intermittent zeal and haphazard success since the days of Governor Simcoe.

In his report, Lord Durham had described the situation facing rural Upper Canadians who desperately needed the facilities for educating their children and who, hopefully, through the education of their children, would become better citizens themselves: "The people may raise enough for their own subsistence and may even have a rude and comfortless plenty, but they can seldom acquire wealth; nor can even wealthy landowners prevent their children from growing up ignorant and boorish, and from occupying a far lower mental, moral and social position than they themselves fill. . . . Even in the most thickly peopled districts there are but few schools, and those of a very inferior character; while the more remote settlements are almost entirely without any."[1]

In the early forties, the common rural schoolhouse was a rough log building about sixteen by twenty feet, heated by an open fireplace. One window on each of three sides let in light, and under it a board was nailed to the wall to serve as a desk. The students sat on benches facing the walls and worked with their slates on this shelf, their backs to the centre of the room. Sometimes the centre space of the room was supplied with benches where the classes moved to recite their lessons to the teacher whose high, crude table-desk faced them. While there were no blackboards or maps, there was a completely miscellaneous assortment of books, as well as goose quill pens to be made and mended by the teacher. Prominent though, an indispensable means of the teacher's authority and symbol of learning itself, was his birch, or if he preferred it, his rawhide tawse. He not only beat the unruly into submission or was "licked" and sent in disgrace from the school section himself, but he taught, or rather terrified into learning, even the youngest of his pupils by regular and relentless use of the birch or the tawse:

Then the recitation—what a scene of confusion and stripes, tears and bellowings. Perhaps it was a column of spellings. A few, fitted by nature with memories adapted for that kind of work, would make their way in triumph to the head of the long, semi-circular class. But woe, woe to the dullards and the dunces, under a regime whose penalty for missing a word would be, very likely, two or three strokes on the tingling fingers or aching palm . . . this proceeding being occasionally varied as some noisy, idling youngster was called up from a back seat to be visited with a still sterner chastisement for some trifling misdemeanor. . . . The place is filled with noise and disorder, rendering study impossible and anything like the cultivation of cheerful and benevolent affections entirely out of the question.[2]

Every second Saturday was usually a holiday, as well as one week in the summer, but at all seasons pupils' attendance was sporadic and, in the case of the boys particularly, determined by the crops and the weather. By the time a boy was nine or ten his strength was too precious an asset at home on the farm to allow the frittering away of his time in school when the ploughing, planting or harvesting were to be done: "The largest scholars that attend our schools are by far the lowest in point of attainment, which shows how sadly the education of that portion of the community, now about to attain the years of manhood and womanhood, has been neglected. In many of our country schools, it is a very common thing to find persons advanced to the age of young men and women commencing to learn the first rudiments."[3]

The process of "getting a school" required everything in patience and humility and almost nothing in qualifications from the teacher. Many school sections engaged men teachers for the winter months and women for the summer when attendance was sure to drop off; the section whose people hired a male teacher all the year around had a certain prestige, but was also suspected of a certain snobbism. A young applicant for a school might be passed for teaching simply on his ability to spell "summons," the favourite test of "Squire Casey," Chairman of Township School Commissions for Adolphustown. Or his examination might take up rather a large portion of the farmer's working day:

My next examination was before the School Superintendent for the County of Hastings, who was also Warden of the County, Mr. William Hutton. I found him ploughing on his farm ... he proposed to examine me en route to the house, ploughing as he went. He gave me for spelling "One fox's head," "Two foxes' heads"—"One lady's bonnet," "Two ladies' bonnets." — But the grand attack was in Grammar, and he asked me to state what part of speech were each of the nine "thats" which were in the following sentence:—"The lady said, in speaking of the word that, that that that that that gentleman parsed was not that that that she requested him to analyze." Having gone through this satisfactorily, I was complimented by the Superintendent, and informed that I was the first Teacher he had examined, who had parsed all the thats correctly, and ... at the House he wrote me out the required Certificate of Qualification.[4]

Once certified, the applicant still had to present himself to the section's parents and get their signatures for the rates payable towards his salary:

Being thus "armed in mail of proof," back again I went to the Trustees of the vacant School Section, and was requested to draw up an Agreement and canvass the section for "signers," which I accordingly did, and succeeded in obtaining the requisite number of twenty-six names, some signing for three dollars, others for two, but more for one, and a few for *half a scholar* ... very few actually signed their names—the bulk of those in the Section "couldn't write very good," but told me to put their names down. . . . The salary for six months at $12 a month, would be $72, from which the estimated amount of the Government Grant, twenty dollars, ($20) being deducted, left $52 for the Section to make up, which averaged $2 per Scholar for the twenty-six signed for, and this was deemed quite a large Bill.[5]

The half-a-scholar signers could send one child for half a term, or two or three for its equivalent in days. "Signing" meant also agreeing to board the teacher: twenty-six signers for a six-month term meant a stay with each of them for a week — a custom designed to fairly spread the expense of the teachers' keep, but certain to insure him a maximum of discomfort and a minimum of privacy.

Understandably, there were almost no efficient teachers and certainly no trained ones—"not more than one in ten fully qualified to instruct the young in the humblest department."[6] Some Superintendents refused to certify "any but strictly sober candidates"—whiskey was as common and as destructive of the schoolmaster as of the labourer in Upper Canada. The teachers were a mixed bag: old soldiers, often disabled physically and mentally; a very few of the stiff-necked Scottish dominie breed; journeying Americans making a hard living out of a very little expertise and always suspect for their use of American texts and devotion to republican ideals; and young girls who could often do no more than read or write themselves: "Cannot you teach a little Grammar? the examiner asked Miss Louisa Whit-comb, in 1843. "I answered 'yes'—doubtfully. He then wrote out a few lines and handed me the paper. It was my Certificate."[7]

Parents' and trustees' ignorance and stinginess more than matched the ineptness of the teachers; many a teaching career ended in dis-missal because the master "gave himself airs" or, worse still, infected the children with dangerous curiosity:

"I might as well tell ye at once that the teacher we intend hiring must be better than the present one. He is a curse to the children of this section, with his grammar and his jography, and all his other fal de rals. Why sir; my son Bill comes home the other night and says he, 'Father, what is grammar?' I says, 'Bill, I never studied gram-mar, and you see how I am able to get along without it. Grammar is no good for ploughing or for cutting up that slash fornent the house.'

So I calls a meeting, and my two colleagues, Thomas Ginty and Edward Crawford, and myself, met at the schoolhouse and dismissed the rascal. . . . 'You don't know grammar?'

Here was the crucial test. . . . 'I don't like grammar and don't know much about it .' . . . The trustee smiled sweetly and said:— 'The school is yours; but remember, no grammar or jography, or out you go'."[8]

The education of the children and of the people of rural Upper Canada had, now, to move; from absolute bed-rock base, the only direction was up. Ryerson was the man for the time and the job. He poured into it everything in him of missionary commitment, of Methodistic organizing, of skill in adapting others' experience to the situations and the people he knew and felt totally competent to lead, and of his own personal ambitions and his enjoyment of learning. At forty-one the sum of his experience in three careers—preaching, teaching and journalism—came into full play in an office where he had power and responsibility without the debilitating, time-losing, public vulnerability to attack, and compulsion to strike back, that he had known as editor of the *Guardian*. While his detractors, George

Brown of the *Globe* chief among them, were still shrieking traitor
and government-toady, he left Canada for several months of travel
and observation overseas. The hostile press added "holiday maker"
and "dilettante idler" to its anti-Ryerson epithets. In fact, during a
trip that lasted from November, 1844, to December, 1845, Ryerson
travelled in a score of countries, observing educational systems, learning from them, and laying the groundwork for his first massive
Report and the drafting of the School Bill of 1846.

He travelled alone. In 1842 Mary Ryerson had borne a son who
had lived only six months; now she and the two girls, Lucilla, eleven
years old and Sophie, eight, stayed in Cobourg, visited and advised
by the Armstrong grandparents, while the head of their house journeyed and trained himself for his new function. Once the misery of
the Atlantic crossing was over, Ryerson was an enthusiastic traveller-
scholar, both restored and stimulated after the battering of the past
year, "painful and humiliating beyond expression."[9] His position now
was far from that of humble Methodist petitioner, or even not-so-
humble unofficial adviser on Upper Canada at the Colonial office.
Now, he travelled with a status which he enjoyed, plentifully supplied
by Lord Aberdeen, the Secretary of State for Foreign Affairs, with
letters of introduction to the British Ambassadors in all the countries
he wished to visit, "including Holland, Belgium, France, Naples,
Florence, Sardinia, Switzerland, Würtemburg, Bavaria and Prussia
. . . . By such kindness and countenance I have no obstruction in my
journeys."[10]

Part of the time, Ryerson travelled with a young Russian, Dunjowski, whom he had met in England and who was both a quick
linguist and an accomplished traveller, with a wide-ranging curiosity
and openness to the novel societies and cultures they encountered.
Dunjowski's companionship greatly enlivened the trip for Ryerson
who, outside of his own interests and responsibilities in religion and
education, was both limited and inhibited. When he met and felt
easy with people of whom he could thoroughly approve, Dr. Gram-
pier, a French Protestant, for instance, he responded with warmth and
vividness; at other times his journal has no lively words. When
impressed or moved, his refuge and resort was the stock ministerial
phrase, heartfelt, no doubt, but impersonally bland. So, in Witten-
berg he stood in Luther's pulpit to pray "that the spirit of the
Reformation might more abundantly rest on me," most surely a
superfluity of which he had no need, and on Vesuvius, with lava
falling all around and burning his face—"God of dreadful majesty,

who art a consuming fire."[11] His days with Dunjowski have by contrast a warm immediacy of impromptu enjoyment.

The worlds Ryerson travelled through external to his education's mission were to be learned, not felt; he went as observer, not participator, both assured of and protected by his unshaken sense of triple identity—Methodist Minister, British Canadian and Educator, each facet knowing its boundaries and functions. What he saw that could be adapted, practically and usefully, to Upper Canada, he carried back in notes and memory. The rest he looked at unengaged, from a position of complete otherness that protected him and channelled his responses to his decided aims and ends. His attitude imposed its limitations upon his experience, but it also had its enormous strength.

He could not, however, train his eyes on schools and schoolmasters to the exclusion of all the rest of Europe's panorama. Paris, in particular, exercised her enormous glamour with an impact that was to take him back and back again until the end of his life.

Paris, March 20, 1845. — It being a holy day, crowds were everywhere; streets for miles were filled with three, and sometimes four lines of carriages of all descriptions. . . . Order was preserved by soldiers and cavalry, stationed at short distances. I never saw such a moving mass of people, embracing, no doubt, every nation in Europe and America. The attractions of the harlequins, jugglers, hucksters, etc., of all descriptions, surpass imagination. I walked to Napoleon's Arch of Triumph; observed the inscriptions and remarkable figures on that elegant and extraordinary structure; ascended to the top, and there enjoyed one of the most magnificent views I ever beheld. . . .[12]

Partly because his mission required a precision of understanding and partly because of the powerful personal attraction, both of Paris and of the learning-challenge, he set himself to learn French. March and April of 1845 he spent sitting in at schools, at the Chamber of Deputies, at Sorbonne lectures, always working at the language, sometimes agonizing over his slowness: "Was strongly talked with for not speaking French; Oh, that God would help me;" at other times rejoicing in hope: "Believe that I shall soon be able to speak. The name of God be praised for His help and blessing! . . . Commenced conversing in French in good earnest."[13] In six weeks of close study he learned the language well enough, not only to understand the Sorbonne lectures he heard, but also to ask the questions and to understand the answers he got regarding educational projects and to converse fairly freely on a social level. He was quick to learn French, as everything else; no subject withstood for long the total commitment and massive concentration he trained on it. From now on basically established in the language, he kept it up for the rest of his life.

From Paris he went through France to Marseilles, then by boat to Genoa, through the major cities of Italy, spending four weeks in Florence, and on to Rome. By the first of August he had come from Venice to Munich, then through Germany to Switzerland, to arrive in Geneva by mid-October. By now he had amassed so much information about European school systems that a month in England, Scotland and Ireland sufficed for a particular look at their Normal and Model Schools. By mid-December of 1845, Ryerson was home again, coming up to Cobourg through New York State and inspecting the Albany Normal School *en route*.

He had organized his observation and research to what he described as a "simple method" and his trip had been no *Wanderjahre,* but a successful, intensive crash course in educational methods: "I have been enabled to proceed, without any loss of time, and without being confused, or confounded by the multitude of objects which have come under my observations—and to classify, and then make a commencement towards digesting the information which I have acquired." There was also a large, fringe benefit of a more personal nature: "I have adopted a similar arrangement in regard to other subjects which have occupied a portion of my attention, relating to the Government, Institutions, Customs, Churches, Morals and other matters of the principal Countries of Central Europe."[14]

The primary purpose of his mission abroad and of all the future work which would issue from it, he defined with total clarity, in accordance with his own temperamental conservatism: "My leading idea has been . . . not only to impart to the public mind the greatest amount of useful knowledge, based upon, and interwoven throughout with sound Christian principles, but to render the Educational System, in its various ramifications and applications, the indirect but powerful, instrument of British Constitutional Government."[15]

Back at home in 1846, drafting his report and the proposed legislation to accompany it, Ryerson had no doubts as to the primary function or the necessary future of Upper Canada's school system. To him education was, quite simply, training for this life; and this life was, in its every facet, a training for the next one: "I am destined to immortality; have but a few years to live in a probationary state, but an eternity to exist."[16] Proper training in this life meant an education which was "not the mere acquisition of certain branches of knowledge, but that instruction and discipline which qualify and dispose the subjects of it for their appropriate duties and employments of life, *as Christians, as persons of business, and also as members of the civil community in which they live.*"[17]

The practical Protestant linking of each aspect of life to the others that had impelled Oliver Cromwell to order his son's teachers to instruct young Richard in his duties to God and in "sound business practices" echoes through time in Ryerson's statement. In his opinion, education *was* training, and the State's exercise of its educational function and responsibility would issue, first of all, in its members' increased efficiency and, therefore, in its own good:

The very end of our being is practical. . . . The age in which we live is likewise eminently practical; and the conditions and interests, the pursuits and duties of our new country, under our free government, are invested with an almost exclusively practical character. Scarcely an individual among us is exempt from the necessity of "living by the sweat of his face." Every man should, therefore, be educated to practice.[18]

Ryerson's Report marshalled a mass of evidence from his travels to support his temporal and national educational goal, which he defines thus:

The branches of knowledge which it is essential that all should understand should be provided for all, and taught to all; should be brought within the reach of the most needy and forced upon the attention of the most careless. The knowledge required for the scientific pursuit of mechanics, agriculture and commerce must needs be provided to an extent corresponding with the demand and the exigencies of the country; while to a mere limited extent are needed facilities for acquiring the higher education of the learned professions.[19]

He had not needed to travel to structure his basic and overall beliefs and policies about the proper and best system for Upper Canada, but in his travels he had assembled imposing authorities to support him. Archbishop Whateley in Ireland, Victor Cousin in France, Horace Mann in Massachusetts, Counsellor Dinter in Prussia—the solemn pronouncements of these men reiterate and give force to Ryerson's own commitment. And his pledged determination was not only to the State, in time; it was also to his understanding of the will of God, in eternity:

We have the brightest light of learning and experience; and we cannot fail of the completest success if every Legislator, and Ruler, and Ecclesiastic, and Inspector, and Trustee, and Parent in the land, will cultivate the spirit and imitate the example of the Prussian School Counsellor Dinter . . . : "I promised God that I would look upon every Prussian peasant child as a being who could complain of me before God, if I did not provide him the best education, as a man and a Christian, which it was possible for me to provide."[20]

Ryerson *had* needed to travel, however, to observe the structuring of educational systems and the operation of the most enlightened pedagogic methods of his time. In these areas he was himself an open-minded student — and he learned well. Enthusiasm for the humane and for the demonstrably successful balance in the pages of his Report; he brushed off the pedantic "Abecedenarians" and "word-mongery" of all kinds with equal impatience — "a parrot or an idiot could do the same thing." He observed both widely and shrewdly and the curriculum he proposed was, for his time, "enriched"; for rural Upper Canada in his time, it was enormously progressive. Art instruction, vocal music, and School Libraries to extend the children's narrow boundaries; the speedy foundation of an Educational Journal to open doors and raise morale among their teachers; investment of funds in art reproductions; and, above all, the investment of funds in a first class teacher-training establishment: for all of these his Report argues with both humanity of outlook and precision of reporting.[21]

When, upon the submission of his Report, he also drafted the legislation that became the School Bill of 1846, he drew on a shrewd knowledge of members of diverse systems and their workings to reform existing legislation, particularly the Baldwin Bill of 1843 which had been liberal in its intentions but inept in its machinery. His goal in this first Bill was one strongly centralized system, a goal which became, as he hoped, a firm base for the further goals to which he was always directed — free schools and compulsory education for all the children.

Ryerson's own office was no longer to be Assistant under Robert Jameson or anyone else. He was to be Chief Superintendent of Schools, appointed and retained at the discretion of the Governor General alone and so outside of Party politics and relatively unthreatened by them. In this he saw himself as a Judge or a Collector of Customs, one whose office's dignity required and *demanded* exemption from factional fighting. His detractors roared disapproval, attributing the direst of autocratic motives to him. "The serfs must receive anything I, their lord and master, may import from the cringing subjects of despotic monarchies," was, cried the *Globe,* Ryerson's stance.[22]

By the terms of the Bill, the Superintendent was to distribute the Legislative grants to the district councils, supervise all school officers, choose and recommend approved texts, direct the Normal School when it became established, draw up plans for schoolhouses and furniture, generally be the source of educational information for the entire province and report annually to the Governor General.[23] The act proposed an advisory board of six members appointed by the Governor General, to help manage the affairs and advise on the questions that the Superintendent "should submit to it."[24] For all this, the Chief Superintendent was to receive a salary "not to exceed £500 currency per annum" and "contingent expenses" and to be allowed a salary of £175 for a clerk.[25] Ryerson wrote in for himself the financial power and he held the public purse. He knew the people out in the country, who would be the trustees, hiring the teachers and locally running the schools, and he intended to use to the full this strongest of all levers on them.

The sub-headings of the Act, 9th Victoria, passed in May, 1846, deal with the specific structure of an entire system: a Normal School for teacher training; Educational duties of Municipal counties, including the appointing of District Superintendents; the duties of these men and of the legally named "School Visitors"—the clergy, judges and municipal officials who were licensed and encouraged to lend support and status to the schools and to be among the examiners of both students and teachers; the formation of School Sections and the election of three Trustees from each, one to retire annually; the certification and duties of teachers; the establishment of Model Schools which were to offer not so much the vocational training that Ryerson had admired in counterparts abroad but "gratuitous instruction . . . to all Teachers of Common Schools within the district."[26]

Ryerson devised, adapted from the old, promoted and administered with incessant strength and energy, a system that turned out to *work.* Mr. Draper, who shepherded the Bill of 1846 through Parliament, had been a strong ally before now; he and Ryerson had understood each other very well in the months between Lord Sydenham's death and Ryerson's letters vindicating Lord Metcalfe. Since 1845, Ryerson had also had another priceless asset—his £175 clerk was Mr. J. G. Hodgins, a young man who had studied under him at Cobourg and had shown himself there to be so interested in education that Ryerson had marked him for the future. In 1845 Hodgins went to Dublin, sent there by Ryerson to attend the Normal School in preparation for becoming Headmaster of the one hopefully to be founded in Upper Canada. When the Bill of 1846 was passed, Hodgins was still in Dublin; plans were changed to allow him to be Ryerson's full-time clerk and assistant. Mr. T. J. Robertson, one of the masters of the Dublin school, came to Canada to be first Headmaster in the Normal School which began classes in November of 1847.

This teacher-training school was a cornerstone of Ryerson's plan; in every country he had seen evidence of the need for such institutions. In Prussia, particularly, he saw evidence, both of the solid achievements of well-trained teachers, and of the strength of a system which had given to its teachers a professional status and dignity. Nothing Ryerson ever did for education was more valuable than his subsequent constant insistence on the dignity of teaching as a profession—on both the rights and the responsibilities of those who taught. His very strong sense of the prime importance of his own office, and his constant insistence on its dignity reflected beneficially on every level of the system beneath him, as he tirelesly urged both training and prestige for teachers:

The best plans of instruction cannot be executed except by the instrumentality of good Teachers; and the State has done nothing for popular education, if it does not watch that those who devote themselves to teaching be well prepared. . . . In all Countries where School Teachers are regularly trained, the profession of teaching holds a high rank in public estimation. . . . Thus the infant and youthful mind of a country, by the law of public opinion itself, is rescued from the nameless evils arising from the ignorance and pernicious examples of incompetent and immoral Teachers. . . . School Teachers will respect themselves, and be respected as other professional men.[27]

Both the Report and the Act raised screaming outcries from the anti-Ryerson faction, spearheaded by the *Globe's* vituperation: "So crooked, so visionary a man . . . he, who sold himself to the late Administration would have readily brought all the youth of Canada to the same market and placed them under the domination of an arbitrary coercive power. He had sold their fathers for pay, why not sell the sons also?" If not downright evil, Ryerson's policies and pronouncements were at best, to his opponents, stupid—"All bunkum, Dr. Ryerson,"[28] jeered the *Globe*.

The Report's "awful disclosures" and its indebtedness to the Prussian system were the cause of the greatest outcry: "It was represented that I had plotted a Prussian school despotism for free Canada, and that I was forcing upon the country a system in which the last spark of Canadian liberty would be extinguished, and Canadian youth would be educated as slaves."[29]

When the Act came into effect a part of the clamour became official opposition. The Gore District Council, with classic near-sightedness, petitioned the Legislative Assembly against the Normal School:

However well adapted such an Institution might be to the wants of the old and densely populated Countries of Europe, they are . . . altogether unsuited to a Country like Upper Canada, where a young man of such excellent character, as a candidate is required to be . . . to enter a Normal School . . . and having the advantage of a good education besides, need only turn to the right hand, or to the left, to make his services much more agreeable and profitable to himself, than in the drudgery of a Common School, at a salary of Twenty-nine Pounds (£29) per annum . . . nor do your Memorialists hope to provide qualified Teachers by any other means, in the present circumstances of the Country, than by securing, as heretofore, the services of those, whose Physical Disabilities from age, render this mode of obtaining a livelihood the only one suited to their Decaying Energies, or by employing such of the newly arrived Emigrants, as are qualified, for Common School Teachers, year by year as they come among us, and who will adopt this as a means of temporary support, until their character and abilities are known, and turned to better account for themselves.[30]

Ryerson's answer to the obstructionists was given in a direct appeal to the people, in a speaking tour that was the second major missionary enterprise of his career. Absolutely determined that he personally would direct public opinion to its own future good—the education of the children—and, incidentally, to an acceptance of his will and authority in educational matters, he travelled the roads of Upper Canada for ten weeks in the fall of 1847, visiting each of its twenty-one School Districts. It was the best time of year to travel the rural roads, as he had learned long ago; far more days were glowing with sun and the glory of the hard maples than grey and raw with rain. And the roads would remain passable. It was also, as he well knew, the season to draw the biggest crowds. The harvest was over, farm work had slackened off, there was a festival air in the beginnings of Fall Fairs in the towns and villages and Harvest Home services in the churches—a mellowing, for a short time, of the people, to match the golden autumn of the land.

In his Report Ryerson had stongly advocated Teachers' Conventions as he had seen them in France and Germany, for the professional improvement and group encouragement they provided. Now, he called a two-day convention in each district. The days were given to discussion of the School Act with all those concerned in its working—teachers, trustees, School Visitors and the District Superintendents. These sessions might be expected to be useful innovations; they pale in importance, however, beside each convention's *Great Occasion,* Dr. Ryerson's public lecture of the evening in between.

The people came on foot or in their rigs, down roads that had not long been more than trails or tracks, to some frame meeting-house, a hall, or a church, or sometimes to a Court House. Many men and a few women filled the hard benches in the yellow kerosene light and the room took on their expectancy, a compound of respect, curiosity and the built-in skepticism of people whose present livelihood and future hopes had always seemed to depend far more on the saving of pennies than on their spending, no matter how high-minded the cause. Usually the Warden of the County, or the High Sheriff, was chairman, his officialdom establishing the occasion's importance and solemnity.

Ryerson knew all these people as well as any man in the land—ignorant parents and progressive ones, suspicious trustees, hopeful or beaten teachers, paid District Superintendents and privileged School Visitors—the uninformed public and the few influential gentry, friends, opponents and neutrals, the generation and the children of the generation he had first preached to, and all the newcomers who had joined them since.

At forty-four his face and figure commanded the confidence that he himself felt; besides that, "Dr. Ryerson" was known by hearsay to everyone in the province, even if to some his reputation was notorious. But even these began to be convinced that for the job to be done in education he was the only man, when they heard the speech that he gave over and over again, on every one of these occasions—"The Importance of Education to an Agricultural People." For in it he elevated the farmers to be "*the* people of Canada," and in so doing he gave his hearers an assurance of dignity that they badly needed to possess. Theirs was not to be a supportive place in the economy, he told them, for "the commercial and manufacturing interests are mere offshoots of the agricultural . . . magnify them as you may, they will be small fractions of the mass, depending both for their character and existence upon the agricultural population."[31]

For nearly a century to come, Ryerson's words were true, as the fortunes of a long line of politicians testified after him, rising or falling by the success of their appeal for the farmers' votes: "Our Counties will give laws to Towns, and not Towns to Counties; and whether patriotism or faction, prevail in the councils of the Government, or, whether quietness, or commotion, reign throughout the land, will depend upon the farmer of Canada; and they will be the arbiters, whoever may be the originators of our Country's destinies."[32]

The Superintendent spoke for nearly two hours on these occasions, from a text that combined the persuasive powers of the journalistic and pulpit rhetoric that he knew so well, with the most practical outlines of ways and means. He wrote to Hodgins of all the audiences' "deepest attention"; at his climactic appeal, they cheered. Then he spoke with emotion, as "the Son of a Canadian farmer," "most fervently desirous of conferring upon the rising and coming generation of Canada, advantages which the Country at large could not afford to agricultural youth in my own school-boy days."[33]

This was Ryerson's keynote speech, and it is both a moving and a significant document in the history of Upper Canada. In it Ryerson persuaded his listeners, individually and in the group, of their dignity, their social coherence, and of a purpose that reached beyond the narrow, restrictive present and yet was neither as far-off nor as elusive as their religious eternities. His goal—and he persuaded them that it was their goal too—glowed, not with mystery, but with a shining practicality that seemed, and was, achievable—beyond today to a tomorrow that would be, for their children, far more spacious. "It becomes us especially to leave to those who are growing up around us, and those who succeed us, the legacy—the priceless legacy of institutions and means of education suitable to the wants, competition and progress of their age and Country."[34]

The tour was a total success. Accidents of weather and the discomforts and inadequacies of the stage coaches and their routes notwithstanding, the trip was Ryerson's "Roman triumph of the backwoods":

My journey from London to Goderich and back again was through hail, snow and rain from above, and an almost uninterrupted sea of mud beneath,—such as I never passed through for so great a distance. But I have no reason to regret the exposure, and fatigues of the journey—having fully accomplished the objects of it. . . . Everywhere there is a loud call for a repetition of such visits. I expect I shall have to follow them up in future years.[35]

This was Egerton Ryerson's high point, the time in his life when all his convictions and all his past experiences came together to generate a sure power to direct and to serve the interests of the people. As he experienced the warmth of acclaim, finding it "affecting in some instances, to witness the grateful feelings of the people,"[36] he felt no doubts whatever about his preeminent ability to follow through with the achievement he promised them. Nor, indeed, had he any reason for doubt—for these people's purposes, in the bed-rock building stage of an educational system, Ryerson was as competent as he became all-powerful.

Chapter 9

Development and Siege

True and powerful in its appeal as was Egerton Ryerson's "I am the son of a Canadian Farmer," its truth had other connotations for him than for most of his hearers. He knew them, he was of them and sure of his role among them. But he also belonged by birth and tradition to the Loyalists who were, for him, a natural Canadian aristocracy, not of privilege, but of status and responsibility. When Ryerson spoke of education for a a "Free" People, he meant a people who were self-determining within British Constitutional Freedom, as Canadians, in principle, now were; he also meant equal before God and in law. The Free Education towards which, from the beginning of his Superintendency, he was driving his Reports and their legislation, he intended to provide a basic equality of opportunity to all. This, how-ever, by no means entirely replaced the parents' responsibilities, or opportunities, to find and provide the best possible education for their children as Ryerson himself intended to do—outside of any public system when necessary. Unlike some vociferous opponents, he was not afraid of a levelling down in society because of a free and standardized system of education, partly because all around him there had always been everything crying to be built up, partly because confidence and optimism were a part of his time and of his belief, and partly because he assumed that there would always be an educated élite. And if he could manage it, his children would be among its numbers.

Eighteenth-century Methodism was rooted in him, its essential message hope. Wesley's doctrine was bright indeed compared to Calvin's, though in the mouths of its preachers gloom and doom were often as prominent. To the early Methodist, though it was true that man was sinful and lost, he only remained lost through his own blind wilfulness; his individual dignity was abundantly evidenced by the plan and the means given him by God for his salvation. Impossible as was perfection for him in this life, he had reason and hope, through both faith *and* works, to train himself towards it in the next. Meanwhile, he shared most fully in that strong current of eighteenth-century thought which gave a sure and certain stature to every human being.

John Wesley himself was a very direct influence for Ryerson as he matured in habits of mind and in experience. All the North American saddle-bag preachers patterned themselves on the leader and his ministry, finding symbols of their own commitments in his life and mission. In the early days of the century they had all seemed close to Wesley in time and in contact with Coke and Asbury, his American bishops. Ryerson, however, connected with John Wesley at far more points than most. Like Wesley, he was a life-long scholar: study, as he said, was his "meat and drink."[1] The education of the people he preached to had been a part of Wesley's province as it was with Ryerson. Only a few of his North American colleagues had gone to England again and again as he had, had preached in Wesley's Chapel or had seen in his house and study the evidences of the scholar-gentleman as well as the humble itinerant. Though events and personalities forced the Canadians out of sympathy with both Anglicans and British Wesleyans, Ryerson himself might gladly have kept, if he could, the impossible balance that John Wesley achieved in his lifetime—to be surely of the Methodists, but also "in connexion with" the Established Church of England.

Life and events in eighteenth- and nineteenth-century North America forced some strange coats on their wearers; of Franklin, and Lincoln, the two American leaders Ryerson mentions with admiration, he is himself far closer to Franklin, though his Methodism would seem to set him worlds apart from Benjamin's genial ease of spirit. The dominant influences on him were of both the British and the North American eighteenth-century. Like Franklin he was, above all, efficient in several disparate worlds, with a chameleon-like ability to adapt to the exigencies of any occasion that might present itself. He put on and took off "the homespun" as the times demanded, to make maximum contact with the various elements of a heterogeneous society with a seeming ease that was maddening to many of his countrymen, and mysterious to most of the English civil servants, politicians and government officials with whom he dealt.

Egerton Ryerson and his family often felt the strain of his balance among the worlds that claimed him. For his own children, he wanted both social status and educational superiority. John Wesley had not relinquished either the habits or the accoutrements of a gentleman-scholar to become a Methodist—why should his followers in time? Certainly personal ambitions played their part too. Social slights at home rankled, the violence of factional feeling against him had left scars, particularly on a man who had a strong sense of his own worth and dignity and who was treated with great respect wherever he went abroad. Then too, as he grew older, Ryerson was more aware of his own pride in his Loyalist background, sometimes militantly voluble about it to the edge of defensiveness. He always remembered John Strachan's early imputations of disloyalty and republicanism to the Methodists and they always rankled.

In 1847, the year after his European tour, Mary Ryerson had a son, Charles Egerton. His birth delighted them both, particularly after the sadness of their first boy baby's death. Ryerson looked forward to Charley's education with a special patriarchal anxiety for the one who would bear the family name. Meanwhile Lucilla and Sophia were to be educated in the manner most fitting for the best young ladies of the day. Many and cutting were the comments of fellow Methodists when Lucilla, at about age ten, was sent to a private school which taught dancing. Her going to a social function given by Lady Elgin at Government House was publicly and loudly deplored at the Methodist Conference and her father had to make a speech in defence of his daughter's presence at what had been a Christmas-tree party for children. These were mere whispers of disapproval, however, in comparison to the storm raised, and not only by Methodists, when he sent Lucilla in her teens to a Montreal convent to learn French. Ryerson never allowed himself to lose the French he had learned with such a mixture of misery and success in Paris in 1845. For him, a knowledge of the French language was the hallmark of the educated, cultivated mind, and he intended that for each of his children. With it went, hopefully, a first-hand familiarity with European, especially French, culture and civilization.

While the nuisance hounds of the press in both Toronto and Montreal were still yapping their choruses of anti-Romish prejudice and personal spite, Lucilla became ill. She came home to Toronto to die of consumption at the age of seventeen, in 1849. No child of Hannah Aikman, "the wife of my youth," remained.

In a day and a society permeated by a "sex equals sin" ethic, only grudgingly mitigated by St. Paul's "better to marry than burn," Egerton and Mary Ryerson lived together and probably got along as well together as most couples. Mary was a plain and pious woman, "industrious, economical, has excellent judgment in buying things both to wear and eat & a good housekeeper."[2] She shared her husband's Methodism and she was both happy and proud to be the wife of a leading clergyman. But her social ambitions went no further than the Parsonage and in or out of it, her element, she had no social glitter. She neither shared nor sympathized with Egerton's real intellectualism or his traveller's eagerness for new worlds to see; her world was her home, her church, her children and family connections. Out of her circle she was uncomfortable and awkward. Her time in England with Egerton in '36 and '37 had been duty, not pleasure. She never went again. In public they both satisfied the roles that they expected of themselves and that convention expected of them—the eminent Dr. Ryerson and his competent and dutiful wife. In private, Mary Ryerson nagged Egerton about the little things and Egerton was unblinkingly arbitrary about the big ones.

Although Ryerson's confidence in his own planning for Upper Canadian education never wavered, his policies were attacked step by step as he made them in the first decade of his holding of office. He had succeeded, as far as any man could do so, in putting his office and his position in it above the pressures and the changes of party politics. However, in 1848, just after the Baldwin-Lafontaine administration was formed, he came again under serious attack—"Will any man, except a few of his own clique, say that Egerton Ryerson should be Superintendent under a Liberal Government?"[3] The next year was one of rioting and unrest, when the Governor General was mobbed and the Parliament Buildings burned. The Legislature met in Montreal and, of course, the Education Office for Upper Canada was in Toronto. The School Bill which Ryerson had drafted, was revised before its presentation in the Legislature by the Hon. Malcolm Cameron, and passed through Parliament. Its revision had, in effect, destroyed its essential provisions.[4] Ryerson wrote a lengthy analysis of the revised Bill, damning its ineptness clause by clause. He also declared that he would resign rather than try to administer it. He got the support he demanded; the Government did not bring the Bill into operation and Ryerson drafted a new bill for the session of 1850.

Numbers of strands of circumstances combined at this time to give the public the kind of confidence in Ryerson as their Educator that he had in himself. The Governor General, Lord Elgin, came out strongly for education and for Ryerson. Elgin was a genial man who travelled to let the people see him; he had succeeded in a variety of posts as a Colonial administrator, he seemed really to enjoy Canada and Canadians, and they reciprocated enthusiastically. Ryerson enjoyed his favour and appreciated his influence. Then too, the fifties were boom years for Upper Canada. Farmers tasted a heady reward for their labours when the price of wheat rose and rose again, going as high as an unprecedented $11.75 a bushel. The dignity of a sound and a useful education for all their children which Ryerson had offered them became a part of the people's pride in their time and place. The present was relatively golden and the country's future must be golden too. In these years public opinion swung with great rapidity towards a system of free schooling, though Ryerson was too clever to push it too fast. In 1850 he contented himself with securing legislation giving trustees the option of free schools and the power to enforce taxation for their support.

Toronto had been a stronghold against free schools. "We cannot deprive a man of the right and the responsibility of educating his own children" and "We should not be taxed to educate the children of others" were equal rallying cries. Early in 1851, a committee of the Toronto School Board came out strongly for free schools because of their finding that more than three thousand children were roaming the streets, growing up with no education of any kind and open to all the dangerous, sordid and anti-social influences that threaten the urban poor. The *Globe* which, in 1848, had been rabidly against free schools had changed its tune by 1851: "We are glad to observe that the plan of free common schools has been adopted at the recent annual meetings in very many school sections throughout Upper Canada .... Public money employed in educating the masses is a most profitable investment, and we hope the day will soon be when a good education is open to every child in the country."[5]

Grudgingly, gradually, but unmistakably, George Brown of the *Globe* recognized and admitted Ryerson's talents too, as he editorially deplored the legislative haggling surrounding a proposed increase in the Superintendent's salary from £375 to £500 annually: "We are no admirers of Egerton Ryerson, and we have always thought, and we think still, that the present ministry should have turned him out neck and crop the moment they got into power; but we are free to admit that he is a man of very great talent, who, at any mercantile or professional business he might engage in, would readily make five hundred pounds a year, and we do think that this sum is as little as could be assigned to an office of such high public importance."[6]

In October of 1850, Ryerson went to England to order and to buy books and maps for schoolrooms and libraries, to consult with educationalists, and to lobby once again against Bishop Strachan in the wearisome case of the settlement of the Clergy Reserves. This was his fifth trip across, an eleven-day voyage and a far cry from the old pre-steam three-week ordeal. Ryerson never did become a good sailor, however; he was sick seven days of this voyage. On the same ship travelled a letter about him written by Lord Elgin to Earl Grey, Secretary of State for the colonies. Grey was Lady Elgin's uncle, a family connection to whom Elgin wrote frankly and informally:

Toronto, Oct. 11, 1850.

My Dear Grey:

By this mail one of the ablest men in Canada goes to England, the Revd Dr Ryerson, Superintendent General of Education in Upper Canada. I should be glad if you could see him—He is accused by many of being somewhat cunning which is not altogether improbable . . . . I believe that he knows as much of Canada as any man and I should be glad if you heard of his opinion, especially on the Clergy Reserves.[7]

Duly entertained by Earl Grey, Ryerson even established for himself a certain social eminence—and that in spite of the legendary convivial brilliance of his fellow dinner-guest, John A. Macdonald:

Nov. 15/50

My Dear Elgin:

Since I last wrote you I have seen both Mr. Macdonald & Dr Ryerson & I have had them to dinner to meet Lord Lansdowne & C. Wood wh. I think has pleased them much—Dr Ryerson strikes me as being a very superior man. . . .[8]

Earl Grey busied himself with practical aid as well as social encouragement: through him, Ryerson was able to buy the books and schoolroom equipment he wished at a forty-three per cent discount. Lord Lansdowne, Chairman of Britain's Privy Council Committee on Education, followed up his meeting with Ryerson by an interview; after hearing Ryerson's explanation of the aims and structure of Upper Canada's school system, he lamented that it could not be introduced to England: "I cannot conceive a greater blessing to England than the introduction into it of the Canadian school system."[9]

Ryerson stayed overseas eight months, not the four he had planned, but there was no settlement of the Clergy Reserves question. In fact, in the face of strong opposition the proposed Bill was not even brought to the Houses of Parliament. But twenty years' experience had armoured him against disillusion. At this point, though he had not lost his conviction as to the justice of his cause, he had certainly developed a seasoned negotiator's love for the game of diplomacy itself and for his own part in the moves of the game. Besides, he had been able to spend time in Paris, and he had found once again, with great satisfaction, that he could pick up his French quickly enough to understand lectures at the University and speakers in the Chamber of Deputies. He even stretched the delay a bit to attend the Great Exhibition, "the grandest of all grand affairs I ever witnessed. I had place near the centre, within a few feet of the 'Iron Duke' "[10]

At home, Mary Ryerson ran the family competently and Hodgins ran the shop—deputy-minister, executive assistant, private secretary and friend. With a clerk or two he did all the work of the Department while Ryerson was away. Beyond that he reported and assessed at length all the other matters which engaged his Chief—Methodism, politics, the Normal School, Victoria College, the University Question—and, of course, the welfare of the Ryerson family. In the mid-fifties, Hodgins turned from the Methodist to the Anglican church, a diversion of loyalties rather fortunate when it came, forestalling some fraction of the ever-present criticism of the Education Office as a Methodist preserve. But Methodism, like all the rest of Ryerson's affairs, was Hodgins' province when the Superintendent travelled; in clerical matters as in all else his mixture of efficiency, deference and initiative ably supported Ryerson's interests, both public and private.

Ryerson's practicality also served their relationship well. Hodgins was a young man with ambitions and the needs of a growing family to attend to. Ryerson neither condescended to him, underestimated his monetary value, nor kept him interminably office-bound. Hodgins travelled many times as Deputy after the extended mission to Ireland which had begun his appointment. In 1855, to the satisfaction of both men, he was formally appointed Deputy Superintendent, his salary doubled, from £225 to £450 yearly.

In the decade of the fifties, Ryerson and Hodgins administered hundreds of schools, already teaching almost three hundred thousand children. All the Government money for them, as well as special sums such as the £15,000 grant for Normal School Buildings, was banked and disbursed in Ryerson's name. Since 1848 they had published the *Journal of Education*, a hopeful agent for the raising of teachers' morale and standards and for the spreading of information and interest about all educational matters throughout the province. They looked after the choosing and buying of books and equipment for Public Libraries and Schools and ran a Book Depository which supplied these, at cost, to local Boards.

Every year, Ryerson wrote a vast report of his activities, sometimes running to three hundred pages. Besides all this, his regular office correspondence averaged six hundred letters a month. In 1853 he toured all of his districts for a second time, judging that the climate of opinion was closer and closer to readiness for a Free School Law, that his presence would accelerate the movement for it—and being proved right in his surmises. Even in the dead of winter, the response was more enthusiastic and more informed than was his first tour. A marvellous advance in the attitude of the people, he called it, "a great enthusiasm evinced," "adopting in every instance almost unanimously resolutions in favour of a *free school law*."[11]

He was gratified to hear them cheer as they had before when they saw him and heard him speak, and their support made the eventual legislating of his proposals certain. But still nothing in the way of legislation could be achieved without controversy. Just now the inflammable question of Separate Schools raged interminably in the press, in parliament and among the factions of the people, sometimes so violently that the entire budding educational system was in danger of cracking apart. Essentially Ryerson's policy had always been to grant the fewest possible concessions to sectarians and he always saw the Separate School question as an unsightly and possibly dangerous crack in the system he so proudly promoted.

In his first report, in 1847, he had declared himself "far from advocating the establishment of denominational schools; but I was not prepared to condemn what had been unanimously sanctioned by two consecutive Parliaments."[12] Almost twenty years later, when the public was caught up in the pre-Confederation enthusiasm for unity, Ryerson elaborated and defended a position that he had always seen as valid. With Ryersonian realism, however, he had likewise recognized that it was inopportune, politically obtuse, and impossible to maintain:

The efforts to establish and extend Separate Schools, although often energetic and made at great sacrifice, are a struggle against the interests of a Canadian society, against the necessities of a sparsely populated country, against the social and political interest of the parents and youth separated from their fellow-citizens. . . . If the Legislature finds it necessary to legislate on the Separate School question again, I pray that it will abolish the Separate School law altogether . . . .[13]

Ryerson and John A. Macdonald understood each other very well. When, in 1855, John A. was seeing the Taché Bill through the Legislature, a Bill whose provisions were exclusively for Roman Catholic Separate Schools and therefore the subject of bitter wranglings, he wrote to Ryerson as one political realist to another:

I need not point out to your suggestive mind that in any article written by you on the subject it is politic to press two points on the public attention: 1st, that the Bill will not, as you say, injuriously affect the Common School System. This is for the people at large. 2nd, that the Bill is a substantial boon to the Roman Catholics. This is to keep them in good humour.[14]

In fact Ryerson's attitude to Roman Catholics and their schools was in part compounded of necessity and expediency, the giving way in lesser things to achieve the greater, for which he quoted solid Biblical backing in the words of Paul to the Romans, "in necessary things unity, in non-essentials liberty, in all things charity."[15] In part he also condescended to the Church of Rome from a height of Methodist security as unscalable and impregnable as John Strachan's tower-position against the Methodists. He looked upon Roman Catholics rather in pity than in anger, as beings mistakenly caught in the "superstitions of popery," and the tyrannies of ecclesiastical authoritarianism. He, of course, and all the host of Protestants with him were fortunate and free, close to the Bible, *the* word of God, "the only safeguard of civil liberty," the only source of true religion, and therefore—close to God himself. "From my travels and experience in Europe, I had formed the opinion that witnessing what appeared to me the trivial ceremonies and customs of the Church of Rome would tend to confirm, rather than unsettle the faith of a well instructed Protestant."[16]

Ryerson's attitude was a refinement of the ordinary current Protestant Upper Canadian attitude of the day. He had civil relationships with many Catholics, priests and prelates, and cordial ones with a few, like Bishop Lynch who sent him port wine to cure a series of boils: "His Lordship said when he went to Lower Canada, he found his *Irish* habit of poor living exchanged for the French custom of having wine three times a day, & stated the beneficial effects of it upon his nervous & general system. He strongly urged me to take wine more freely, & live on more hearty foods. . . . Today a dozen bottles were sent with his Lordship's compliments; and on opening a bottle, I found it to be the best and most invigorating Port that I have tasted in a long time." [17] The ordinary man in the Methodist pew deplored all

Roman Catholics and all port wine with impartial intolerance and passion.

In the mid-fifties, Ryerson's rooted antipathy to any ministerial authority which smacked of the power of the Roman Catholic priesthood, together with a doctrinal liberality which ran counter to the beliefs of the hard-line Methodists of the Canadian Conference, plunged him into internal church controversy. He came out at his sternest and strongest against the power of ministers to expel members from the Methodist Church for non-attendance at mid-weekly "Class Meetings" and in favour of the rights and privileges of all baptized children within the church. When, at Conference in Belleville, the resolutions he moved were rejected by a large majority of his fellow clergy, he wrote to Dr. Enoch Wood, resigning from the Conference and returning his parchment of ordination. Ryerson had outgrown and outstudied certain literal-minded and restrictive interpretations of the Methodist Discipline. Many of his colleagues had not. Some of them resented his secular power and policies and had hangovers of suspicion about his notoriety as a political turncoat. His brother John, who would certainly have acted as mediator and peacemaker, was off on a Missionary tour of Hudson's Bay. So Egerton Ryerson, for thirty years a minister and leader of Canadian Methodists, became a layman. His rejection by Conference was the bitterest blow of his clerical career: once again, as in the low point of the late thirties, he was pushed toward notions of joining with the Anglican Church.

John Ryerson returned from the North-West. He and many wise, temperate and senior Methodist ministers were appalled at what had been a kind of "packed jury" against his brother. Consequently, Egerton rejoined the Conference in 1855 and both he, personally, and the liberal doctrinal principles for which he argued were vindicated by a large majority vote at the Conference of 1856.

Meanwhile, however, in his fifties the strain of constantly bringing himself up to the mark of passionate engagement in a diverse series of controversies, added to a day-by-day enormous work load, had begun to affect Ryerson's health, both physical and mental. More and more often he had days of blinding headache followed by days of complete physical exhaustion, spells of depression, and times in which he could not preserve his former fighter's calm in the face of attack, but was far too vulnerable to anger or to tears.

Several doctors diagnosed complete physical exhaustion and advised change; his daughter, Sophia, who was nineteen and at the very best age for a finishing educational trip abroad, provided an incentive of usefulness, and in July, 1855, Ryerson set forth with her for six months in Europe. If he needed still more justification in the taking of a holiday—and he did—he was self-commissioned to re-inspect European educational systems to bring himself up to date on their improvements. He planned to buy equipment for the teaching in Upper Canada of art and science, and for the Provincial Educational Museum which was being planned. The government also named him Canada's Honorary Commissioner to the great Paris Exhibition.

Sexual, social and temperamental inhibitions raised high walls between male and female in the nineteenth-century, but sometimes the father-daughter relationship could be a splendid thing. So it was with Egerton Ryerson and Sophia. She was bright and socially graceful; she learned quickly and she was eager to learn. He could go with her into society and situations that intrigued and impressed him and for which he could find no excuse to go alone. A man could be pardoned, even applauded, for wishing to introduce his daughter to the best society or even to attend with her an audience given by the Pope —though it would be well if the Conference did not hear of it—when for himself or for his wife the same activities would be sure to command the gossip-labels of frivolous social climbing, or to be censured as downright sinful. Besides, there was between these two, father and daughter, a clear-eyed depth of love, understanding and frank communication which supported and stimulated them both.[18]

Sophia and her father were fêted wherever they went; by the Governor and Lady Head in Quebec; by Mr. and Mrs. Widder of the Canada Company who stayed at the same Paris hotel; by the Earl and Countess of Grey, who met them in France; and by Lady Grey, their aunt, an eccentric self-exile who lived in Rome and had *conversazioni* for the travelling intelligentsia of Europe. In his life, Egerton Ryerson had many moments of achievement, but socially he had never had moments as sweet as these, when Sophia shone in his eyes before distinguished company and he enjoyed the kind of literate, heterogeneous civilization to which one large, and largely stifled, part of his nature had always aspired. Even a bout of lumbago in Rome was less agonizing to him than it might have been, because he was attended by Dr. Pantelioni, whom he had met at Lady Grey's *soirées*, a doctor who was "one of the most generally read and enlightened men I had met with, . . . who attended me daily for three weeks, and never charged me more than a dollar a visit."[19]

Part of Sophia's time was spent at a Protestant French school in Paris, for her father was determined that she should learn and keep the French language, preferably without the storm that had attended Lucilla's enrollment at the convent in Montreal. Ryerson himself spent a good part of his time in the choosing of exhibits and art reproductions for the Museum-to-be and in negotiating for their sale and transfer.[20] He also renewed his friendship of ten years before with Dunjowski, who had since become a Roman Catholic missionary and who provided him with valuable introductions to officials in Florence and Rome. In Florence he listened to Garibaldi in the Italian Legislature—"a skilful party leader, but no statesman."

The travellers stayed a month more than they had planned and arrived in Toronto early in the spring of 1856, Ryerson's health much improved, Sophia's French quite accomplished and each of them so well satisfied with the other as a travelling companion that they repeated the experience when Ryerson went over again to hire a Normal School master in the fall of 1857.

There was one more deep trough in the waves of his fortunes to be ridden out before the decade of the fifties ended, and it was well that Ryerson returned from Europe with a sufficient resurgence of physical stamina to bear it. Late in November, 1855, John Langton had become Provincial Auditor. After some months of digging into the accounts of the Education Office he presented Ryerson with an account of £1,527.7.4 for interest which he, Ryerson, had personally received on public money booked in his name. Langton's accounting was valid enough, though the total was an overcharge of about two hundred pounds. Ryerson's practice was, however, valid too, according to the current way of handling public money, so that the bank paid no interest to the Government, but only to the individuals in whose accounts the government-money was deposited. Furthermore, Ryerson had discussed his using of the interest money with three members of Parliament—Hincks, Macdonald and MacNab. Each one had approved, verbally—but there was no official correspondence on the subject. Langton's position as an instigator of the investigation was weakened by his personal antagonism to Ryerson, whom he called the "Pope of Methodism," "my Jesuitical friend" and by his gloating over the situation: "The great father of lies himself is not up to more cunning dodges than my reverend friend."[21] For his part, Ryerson looked poorly in the defensive position which he had to adopt; he equated the interest money with expenses accrued during his Superintendency, declared himself determined to pay the former and sent to the Government an itemized Bill for the latter. His claims were allowed: "In the view of the Government of the day, therefore, the offence against equity was so much less than that against law that the offender emerged with a balance of £177.15 to his credit."[22]

However much the settlement announced a recognition of error on both sides rather than guilt on one, Ryerson, his brothers and his family had to live, and somehow hold their heads up, through a nasty, demeaning and sordid situation. Battle they were used to, and its blood and bruises—but squalid dirt was something new and far harder to bear. It became especially so when the Conference of 1858, certainly given over to evangelical rigour if not to self-righteous cant, expelled Edwy from the ministry and the church, disciplined John after an investigation of his character, leaving him without a station for a year, and ignored Egerton in all its business, its reports and committees. John Borland, minister of the Toronto Adelaide Street Church, also took the occasion to discipline the private life of the backsliding Ryersons, deploring by letter the rumour of Sophia's attendance at a Governor General's Ball, and her parents' absence from prayer meetings. He commented sharply on their faulty attendance at church "but once on each Sabbath day, with exceptions even to this,"[23] and politely, but unmistakably, implied a threat of expulsion: "There are some who do not hesitate to say that such treatment of our Means of grace should be regarded as a Virtual withdrawal from the Church. Nor is it easy to deal with the assertion when we consider that such would unquestionably be the case in reference to a private member."[24]

Sophia remembered and always resented the Methodists' waspish treatment of her father at this time; if she had ever really been of them, she was lost to them from this time on. There was, however, a reality of Methodism—and of humility—in Egerton Ryerson that allowed him to accept the chastisement and to forgive it.[25]

Chapter 10

The Finished Pattern

From 1844 to 1876, all Ryerson's years as Superintendent of Education became steadily more dense with complexities of management, of political implications and of personal considerations. He and Upper Canada had been young and simple together, with boundless resources of energy and potential power for driving ahead to deal with issues that had looked as clear-cut as the cornerstone Methodist choice of sin or salvation. Population, politics, and the accelerating rush of events complicated the progress which had seemed so brightly simple and inevitable. Increasingly the times demanded enormous strides of the men who formed policies and administered affairs.

On his first European tour in 1845, somewhere, as he liked to tell, in a "mountain solitude" among the Alps, Egerton Ryerson had dreamed, and planned, an entire, comprehensive School System, joining all education in its benign authority, from the primary school to the university. There and then, at the very beginning, he had tried to consider the province as a whole, "apart from its political-religious dissensions, and to ask what system could be devised to enable it to take its position among the civilized nations of the world." He had come down from his mountain top to adapt his vision to a real world; political-religious dissensions were all too real and stumblingly present. But in thirty years of the growing complications of persuasion and direction, he did achieve the cornerstone of his projected system— Free and Compulsory Primary Schooling for all children. And that achievement, clause by clause and law by law, was based on an even greater achievement, the persuasion of the people of the province to a belief in education as a primary responsibility of the government, "the first charge on the wealth of the province."[1]

As Wesley for Methodism, Ryerson carried the blueprint for Ontario's education in his head and again like Wesley, his success lay in his power with the ordinary people. He had the power to persuade them by his rhetoric, to give them pride in their educational system. Then he pushed their pride to its practical application by an unrelenting use of his financial lever over all the school sections and trustees— his administering of the funds for school grants. He understood his function as one of paternalistic, benevolent—and total—authority over all the echelons of the system under him. All offices, situations and requests engaged his personal attention, from querulous complaints about costs from trustees, to timid enquiries about School Law from teachers, to the detailed planning of the brick School-Houses that now dotted the country, marking hopefully its civilizing effect in the present and its confidence in the future.

At the same time his power and the entire developing system had to be negotiated legislatively. Political manoeuvrings were constant and unavoidable, though at no time after the earliest years was his own position as Superintendent in jeopardy. Certainly that was not because he lacked critics, for he was constantly a storm centre for controversy, but because at all times, despite the hot contesting of various issues— Separate Schools, or the University question, or the auditing of his books—the work of his department went on uninterrupted, and progress was there for any man to see. Even in the midst of his investigation, John Langton had grudgingly admitted that the Education Office, in the system and the order of its books and in its prompt accountings, should be a model for all government departments.

Efficiency in administration and patience in detail: these were two prime ingredients of Ryerson's success. The third one was the high dignity he set upon his own office, and his insistence that all others accept his evaluation of it. John A. Macdonald captured Ryerson's quiet and unobtrusive exercise of influence for him in the General Election of 1861; it was, as Macdonald acknowledged, "none the less effectual for all that." But Macdonald, after a long association, knew his man, how much he could ask of Ryerson and how to ask it. Sidney Smith, on the other hand, felt the full force of the Superintendent's dignity when he asked for Ryerson's help in canvassing: "I think you must have forgotten that it would be as inconsistent with the avowed character and relations of my office for me to go and canvass in an election as for one of the Judges of the Queen's Bench to do so. I have *never* done so throughout my whole life."[2]

Early in the spring of 1860 Egerton Ryerson finished his third speaking tour around the province's school conventions. Physically, a provincial tour was still a taxing ordeal: roads were better, but they were never good in February and March. And the hazards of the banquet circuit were never greater than in the latter half of the nineteenth century, when the test of hospitality was quantity and variety of food, especially of rich preserves, cakes and pies and it was a compliment to hospitality to call a well-stocked table a "groaning board." Now the Teachers' Conventions were well-established in their traditions. Something of the aura first surrounding "Dr. Ryerson" had been dispelled through years of teachers' contact with his pronouncements in the *Journal of Education*, and of trustees', in his answers to their enquiries and in his dispersal to them of public funds. What had disappeared in awe, however, had more than enough compensation in confidence and in the progress of the people's thought. In 1860 he spoke urging parents to support a Free School Act and to give their children an education that would enable them "to take care and make a proper use of Property that might be left to them."[3] Dr. Ryerson's presence and his speech soundly reinforced a growing confidence among the public in teaching as a profession to be respected. Particularly for their daughters it had become a desirable career with some social status; at the least it was a useful way for a girl to fill up the years between school and marriage, and it conferred both independence and a certain dignity on those who would remain spinsters.

Ryerson was far from being an advanced thinker on the education of women, but as necessity had forced boys and girls together in the early rural schools of the province, so necessity had always dictated the use of young women as primary school teachers. Soon after the founding of the Normal School in Toronto women were admitted, and by 1848 a "female class" was in training there. By 1860, for a farmer to have his daughters "teaching school" commanded, for his family, a definite increase in the community's respect. The teaching young women of rural Upper Canada speedily became an important part of the province's pattern of society. As the decades passed and their numbers increased, while those of young men teachers decreased, women became the foundation-resource of the entire educational system.[4]

Ryerson went straight from this inspection and consolidation of his particular hustings to Quebec City where the University Question was being discussed in answer to a representation made to the government by the Methodist Conference of 1859. He expected to be there a few days only; he was delayed for nearly six weeks by a series of acrimonious disputes and hearings at which the Toronto University men, headed by John Langton, now Vice-Chancellor, and Daniel Wilson,

Professor of History, called his capabilities for office into question and held his lack of formal higher education up to scorn. The main question at issue was, of course, the claim of the denominations and their colleges on public funds and the determination of the University men to keep the funds centred in their hands, for their institution. The building of the great expensive pile of University College had consolidated the resentment and sense of being ill-used into concerted action from denominational colleges. Led by the Methodists, the strongest group among them, they were all—Presbyterians, Baptists, Anglicans and Roman Catholics—in hot pursuit of the "Godless University and College."

The climax of the Quebec session came as Langton, Wilson and Ryerson each defended his position, the latter finally answering the others and defending the position of the colleges in a two-hour speech. It was one of his most notable oratorical efforts, moving some of his hearers to tears and all those on the denominations' side, to cheers. The effort was enormous: "I felt myself as weak as water. . . . I was so depressed & affected the night before & and morning of commencing my defence, that I could not speak without emotion & tears. . . . I did not lie down until five o'clock this morning, made notes for my intended reply. . . ."[5] Weeks of hearings and months of continued negotiation were futile in their outcome; in May, 1863, this bid for increased support was lost to the denominational colleges. In 1868 even small grants were cut off from the denominational colleges and the University of Toronto was left exclusively the recipient of state aid.[6]

To bring himself up to the pitch of public controversy had been, for much of his manhood, a zestful stimulation for Ryerson, particularly when it was conducted through the press, less so when he had to defend a position on a public platform, though this he had not shrunk from. "For more than thirty-five years of my public life my constitution and brain seemed to be equal to any amount of labour which I might impose upon them."[7] In the fifties, his body had warned him of its diminishing ability to bear such strain; now, in his early sixties, he suffered a real breakdown in health, a constant recurrence of the intense headaches which had debilitated him a few years earlier, and some really crucial illness which affected his chest, head and throat. He lost forty pounds, slipping from the corpulence which in his day was considered pleasingly healthy, to a skeletal thinness. Brother John wrote cheerfully—"the loss of a little of your 'fleshy substance' may prove no great calamity,"[8] but Ryerson continued weak and despondent and his family and doctors were alarmed.

In 1860 Sophia had married Edward Harris, one of the sons of Amelia Ryerse Harris, Egerton's first cousin, schoolmate of his childhood and, for most of his life, a respected friend. The engagement and the marriage surprised the Ryersons a little, but Amelia Harris and all her family were eminently desirable as social and family connections. Sophia had often visited Eldon House, their home in London. It was a social centre of the city where Amelia, widowed, presided as hostess and managed the affairs of her family, including the marriages of her seven daughters and three sons, with a strong will, a certain charm and an enormous sense of the family's dignity and substance.

Just two months after the marriage, occurred the greatest Canadian social event of the decade, the visit to Canada of the future King Edward VII. Eldon House itself combined the honour and the peril of his entertainment in London, for all of this first Canadian royal tour was a particularly dizzying experience for hosts and guest. The Harrises were Anglican and their social and intellectual attitudes were far more broadly organized than those of a Methodist parsonage, but they were not broader than Ryerson's own. In fact, it was for this kind of family and this kind of social prestige and assurance that he had educated Sophia. He was all the more shattered, therefore, at a time when his health and his nerves were undermined, to have Sophia come home in 1862, her marriage apparently broken and a legal separation in the offing. The almost unbearable part of the blow was that Sophia was accused of giving offence—Edward Harris had thought himself neglected in favour of her social frivolities.

Ryerson had one recourse in this pit of despondency and physical weakness which, in fact, finally brought him back to a health and strength remarkably close to that of his younger manhood. He reverted to the kind of exercise and recreation that he had taken for granted as a young man and a young preacher. He swam and walked, rode horseback, rowed boats, split wood and went shooting. In time he regained an astonishing degree of fitness. "Between two and three years ago I found it painful labour to walk one mile, I have since walked twelve miles in a day."[9] Paramount in his recovery was the Crusoe's island he had found as his retreat, a sandy, reedy little island sticking out into Long Point Bay on Lake Erie. It had been an extra land grant to his father, Joseph, to compensate for an error in the original acreage given him. When Joseph died in 1854, Egerton alone among the brothers wanted the island whose very existence was threatened year by year as its sand banks slipped and slid into Lake Erie. He and Charley had gone down to Long Point in the late fifties and found it still there, and habitable. For the next twenty years it withstood erosion to be his haven and his Walden, though always he prudently spoke of his plans for the next year's improvements with a conditional "if the bank of the channel remains."

There he was intensely satisfied to carpenter, to garden, and to shoot ducks in season, for the marshy shores of Long Point were famous game-bird territory. Most of all, he enjoyed being alone to read or write or think. On his first trip there after his illness he made a little skiff to row himself back and forth the four miles to Turkey Point, the closest land, or, for a stiffer pull, the thirteen miles to Port Ryerse. Quite often Charley accompanied his father to the island. In his early teens he had a hideous accident there when the load of his gun went through his hand, shattering his forefinger so that the doctor had to saw off the bone "with a shamefully dull saw."[10]

Charley shared many of his father's sporting enthusiasms. At home in Toronto they would row over to the Island and back, in their fifteen and a half foot skiff, often between six o'clock and eight in the morning, or late in the afternoon after school was out and the office closed. Then, as his strength returned, Ryerson was tempted to try longer voyages. At first all alone and then with Charley, he would sail and row from Toronto to Port Dalhousie, with luck making it in about nine hours. There they would find a boat to take them and the skiff through the Welland canal to Port Colborne, and then they would row along the north shore of Lake Erie, the same route by which Joseph Ryerson had come to settle in Canada about seventy years before. Sometimes Egerton alone—sometimes he and Charley—would make forty miles in one day, from the mouth of the Grand River to Port Dover, "taking refreshments and rest at farm houses, and bathing three times during the day."[11] The day after his first such rowing adventure, he was "scarcely conscious of fatigue" and the following day he spoke twice, once to a large outdoor school picnic and again to an evening meeting of teachers and trustees.

The expeditions combined pleasure with pilgrimage. Usually when he came down to the island Ryerson preached a sermon or two in the Woodhouse Methodist Church whose congregation dated from 1800 and in whose graveyard Joseph and Mehetabel Ryerson were now buried. One autumn he boarded for two weeks with the Duncan family who now lived in the long, porticoed white frame house about three miles from Vittoria, "the woodwork of which I, as an amateur carpenter, had finished more than forty years ago."[12] Such occasions gave him great pleasure, marking, for him, a "wheel has come full circle" vindication of all the decisions, all the achievements and all the disappointments of the years between. At these times, he felt free as he had never been free since childhood and the frightening pain in his head which was accompanied by loss of sight and two or three days' complete uselessness, never re-occurred.

He rightly valued such companionship with Charley too, for the boy of whom much was expected was neither the eager nor the quick learner that Sophia had been. Moreover, in her husband's opinion, Mary Ryerson coddled the boy and blocked the development of sound educational habits in him. Ryerson needed to exert over Charley all the influence and all the affection that he could assemble. With a psychological acumen that was far ahead of his time and in advance of his own stern teaching practices, he proceeded to do so—and to succeed.

For all that, everyone but Sophia carped at Ryerson's relaxations in rowing and sport. There were various public complaints about the culpable rashness of a senior official who would insist on rowing about on the lakes in all kinds of wind and weather. And Mary Ryerson herself, though she must have noticed the benefits to her husband's health and spirits, spoke for all the prudent conformers to the Victorian God of Appearances when she complained to Sophia, "I think he's too old for such amusements. Besides I do not think it looks well for a minister to be sporting so much of the time."[13]

However, under the sober clerical garb of the Methodist parson, the spirit of the eighteenth-century sporting gentleman lived and now moved joyfully to the surface. When Ryerson describes his voyages, his garden's abundance on the sheltered island, or his high-stepping horse, Fred, his versatility and his energy of enjoyment make connections with men like Franklin and Jefferson, who busied their minds and talents in many worlds, or like his own father, the Squire, who had signified his sense of his place in the world around him by the confident classical design of the house he built on his sandy farm in Norfolk.[14] Ryerson's rejuvenation of the sixties also connects in memory and in spirit with his youthful satisfaction among the Credit Indians, when he taught them to build and to garden, to cook and to housekeep and felt in himself a sense of the power to change and to civilize far more immediate than any he had known since.

One other great satisfaction Ryerson had at this time of illness was the drawing towards him of Bishop Strachan, now in his eighties and physically frail, but far from frail in mind or spirit. He had always been indefatigably a visitor and comforter of the ill or the bereaved;

he was among the first to present himself at Ryerson's bedside. In such a time and place, with layers of superficial differences peeled away, these two men had minds and spirits which met and mingled very comfortably. For Ryerson the consolation was sweet; there was a strength in Strachan that had forced an equal growth of strength in Ryerson and in this late-blooming recognition he could feel as if perhaps he had measured up to the mark set by his old adversary.

By 1865 Ryerson was working at much of his old pace. Sophia's shaken marriage had found its equilibrium and she was back in her place at Eldon House. Though the pains in his head were a chronic condition to be lived with from now on, he knew the relaxing measures he must take for their prevention or cure and he did save himself a certain amount of office work and of official travel by deputizing Hodgins more and more and trusting in his judgment. When it came time for a provincial tour, however, Ryerson still considered himself the only man for it. In January and February of 1866 he held forty meetings on his fourth tour around the province.

For the first time, these meetings did not repay the gruelling effort. He was impeded and depressed by sleeplessness and an attack of lumbago. It crippled him on January 17 at Cayuga, continued to give him pain for weeks, and certainly gave him unusual impatience with the whole proceeding. "The speaking was miserable," he says of one meeting, "& I felt that my own speaking was not much better than that of others. There did not seem to be a man present, who had a general principle or an elevated thought in his mind."[15] Furthermore, the people did not accept his proposal for consolidating, under township school boards, the rural school sections' boards of three trustees. They were too attached to local power in small areas to be impressed by the argument of more efficient management in large units. Though at the tour's completion he felt encouraged to draft the legislation for township boards, it was too far in advance of its time to have any success. The consolidation of Ontario's rural schools has only recently reached completion.

The monopoly of the Book Depository on the textbook and apparatus supply to the province's primary schools was also under attack at this time. In its beginning, in 1851, it had been an efficient agent in the standardizing of Common School texts—also a persuasive one, in the discount at which it sold its books to the schools. But inevitably, as the province developed, what had seemed paternalistic wisdom began to look like stubborn autocracy, or even the kind of favouritism that Ryerson himself had deplored, thirty years before, in the affairs of the

Family Compact. At this time, George Hodgins and two other men closely connected with the Superintendent's office were making money from textbooks authorized by the Council of Public Instruction, the Superintendent's advisory committee. Mr. Campbell, a publisher, was the chief assailant of the Depository. He united with the ever-eager *Globe* to indict Ryerson's policies and to ridicule Hodgins' Geography text, publicly listing its errors. For the time being the Depository's function and Ryerson's authority withstood the attack and remained unshaken. But from this time on, it was an intermittent issue, for it could be and certainly was argued that its principle ran counter to that of free enterprise, one of the most treasured shibboleths of the nineteenth century.

In 1866 Charley was nineteen, in his father's opinion sufficiently mature and, hopefully, advanced enough in his studies to benefit by a "Grand Tour" abroad as Sophia had done. Ryerson managed an official six-month leave, primarily to buy twelve thousand dollars' worth of school equipment, and to look particularly at American and European institutions for the Deaf and the Dumb. He was allowed an expense grant of $3000, generous by most standards and staggering compared to the conditions of his first tour, when he agreed to find an entire year's expense money himself. Whatever the trip's impression on Charley, it *was*, for his father, a Grand Tour. On ship, he had the Captain's cabin; everywhere he went, old connections and new letters of introduction insured special facilities and gratifying hospitality. As always, Paris was his special pleasure and the hub of his visit. Charley was pushed and prodded into the French that was so much his father's delight. He was also given, as Sophia had been, a taste of everything that could be certified as culturally uplifting and socially circumspect:

Charley is charmed with Paris; he thinks it the most splendid and delightful place possible. We have been at the principal places of interest. . . . We have also been at the principal Theatres—as I wish Charley to see, as you did, one & once of each kind. . . . We went to the Opera once, . . . to the theatre of the Palais Royale to hear and witness the Commedia "La Vie Parisienne"—a most extraordinary and amusing piece. . . . We went also to the Theatre Français to hear a commedie, "Les Plaiders," by Racine, & three of Molière's commedies. . . . We were last night to the largest and finest theatre in Paris. . . . There were 28 Tableaux and 400 performers. . . . We are now done with this sort of thing. . . .[16]

Ryerson was, all his life, hungry for learning. Now he found once again that he commanded the French language to his own entire satisfaction and enjoyment. All the time that he could spare from Charley and from his official mission he spent at the Sorbonne, listening to the professors discuss all subjects with "remarkable freedom" and finding in such lectures "a great pleasure & relief to the mind." His participating delight in Paris as the centre of European civilization was poles apart from its overwhelming reputation as a "City of Sin" in the minds of most of the Canadians he lived among at home.

The two travelled through Italy, came back to England and arrived home shortly before Dominion Day in 1867. Certainly no one occurrence had the dramatic effect on Charley Ryerson that his father wished; there was no sudden Methodist-like conversion to make a driving scholar out of an amiable, easy-going boy who liked far too well, for parental ease of mind, the good life introduced to him. But the accumulation of all the experiences and companionship with his father, his example and his affection did have its stabilizing effect. Charley finished school, college, and law training, married Lily Beatty, a cousin on his mother's side and a "good match," and settled down to a respectable career as a barrister.

Ryerson's contribution to the celebration of Dominion Day was an "Address to the People of Upper Canada," published in July, immediately after his return from Europe. In this pamphlet he stood firmly in the positions to which, after forty years of public service, he felt himself entitled—Canadian, senior statesman, and citizen of the world. He argued for increasing tolerance and wisdom among all the factions and the parties in the country, in the interests of Canada's future advancement.

In particular he argued *against* "the bitter party spirit of the press," "the unscrupulous partisanship of the press and politics," their "moral assassinations" of public men. "In England, the character of public men is regarded as the most precious property of the nation. . . . But in Canada, the language of a partisan press and politician is 'down with the man; execrate and execute the man as a corruptionist and traitor'."[17] Out of his own experience and from the confidence and the distillation of conviction that his career had left with him, he made a convincing case, sombre in its thesis—the "manifest decline in the standing and ability of our public men," but hopeful of a new future for Canada—"raised from a state of colonial subordination to one of affectionate alliance with the mother country."[18]

The School Act of 1871 was Ryerson's major and culminating achievement in Ontario's education. Public opinion had needed to develop through almost thirty years of growth and experience before the Free and Compulsory Education for all the children, which he had always planned, became law. And ironically, but inevitably, even as it was achieved, both Ryerson's power and his usefulness as Superintendent were nearing their end. To look back through the past at his system's progress is to become convinced that he did, as he said he did, see the whole plan at the very beginning of his tenure—even that the plan's achievement made a matching contract with the length of his working years.

The change and growth for which Ryerson had worked like a giant, had, inevitably, brought forth men who would increasingly challenge his policies and finally supplant his power with theirs. He neither felt any pressing need, nor had he any longer the elasticity, to adapt to a new times' new set of demands. At the very beginning, he had put his office above politics, and there it had remained so successfully that for years it was the custom in Parliament for the Leader of the Government to introduce Educational Bills and the Leader of the Opposition to second them. There had been many years when there were no men in the government who were really competent to question Educational policies, much less to direct them. At Teacher's Conventions Ryerson had been the "great law-giver." Even there, he had scarcely ever met a man who was as well-read or as knowledgeable about education as he was himself, until in the sixties the Secondary schools—then called Grammar Schools—began to hire university-trained teachers.

The School Bill of 1871 abolished all rate bills on parents. Since 1850 so many Trustee Boards and ratepayers had voted to establish the free schools allowed them that the final legal move seemed to come as an anticlimax. Parents were now liable to penalties for neglecting to send their children to school and a system of county inspection, carried out by fulltime inspector "experts," was made legal, this again developing from the Act of 1860. The County Inspector, with two or more qualified teachers, constituted a County Licensing Board, with the power to issue second- and third-class certificates to teachers who had not been trained at Normal School, but who passed an examination set by the Council of Public Instruction. This ruling finally set up a uniform qualifying standard for teachers throughout the province. An important initial step towards the financial security within the teaching profession was the beginning of pension-fund payments, compulsory for men and voluntary for women.

There was also an important Grammar School Act of 1871. After several false starts and half-hearted reforms, the High Schools and the Collegiate Institutes of Ontario were given their first strong push into useful vitality and professional efficiency. Probably the Act's most important result was the setting up of standard province-wide entrance examinations which quite speedily buttressed their educational meaning with a broader social one. To have their children "pass the entrance" soon became the basic public signal of a family's self-respect, and before long, responsible and ambitious parents added the developing secondary examination levels—the matriculation examinations—to their requirements of family resources and of their children's competence. "To get the junior matric," the intermediate qualification, or "the senior matric," the highest level of the public system, became part of the province's speech and of its life.

In 1876, after thirty-two years in office as Superintendent, Ryerson retired. A Minister of Education, an elected Member of Parliament, replaced him; the Council of Public Instruction which had been advisory only and quite responsible to Ryerson, was transformed into a Department of Education, staffed by civil servants who were not to be tied to party changes. Ryerson fought through, and won, a final victory over governmental haggling, claiming and getting a full-pay pension. Then at age seventy-three, after fifty years of the public exercise of his time and talents, he was free.

Freedom, but *not* idleness! "Indeed in old age every care should be taken to avoid yielding to lassitude and sloth."[19] Ryerson had been planning the projects of his retirement since his fifties at least. "My plan is, if spared from the age of 60 forward, as long as I have life and strength, to write books for the benefit of my country."[20] He had many books in mind and several of them he wrote—pamphlets really, on Agricultural Economy for the Canadian farmer, on Christian Morals for the Canadian family—even one arguing the morality and legality of marrying one's deceased wife's sister. In this one he supported his friend and colleague, Mr. Morley Punshon, who proposed to do that very thing.

His great literary dream, however, the purpose and the plan of his retirement, was directed towards the writing of *The Loyalists of America and Their Times*. For this work he had planned and read for fifteen years before his retirement, at least as far back as 1860, when he wrote to Sophie: "My present reading and studies are preparatory to what I intend as the chief work (in the way of authorship) of my life. I would rather not do it at all, than not do it in a manner that would do credit to me & give it permanent value."[21] The book took various shapes in his mind: sometimes it expanded to become an entire and comprehensive history of English-speaking peoples. At one time he had certainly finished two volumes on *The Puritans in Old and New England* that he felt would "raise a storm on both sides of the Atlantic"[22] and that, therefore, he hesitated to press towards publication. Undoubtedly the final, published, two-volume, thousand page version was only a fraction of the manuscript he had produced in years of reading and in the precious holiday writing-times at his Long Point cabin.

Finally, for six months after his retirement he experienced, in the British Museum, the scholar's life he had dreamed of through years of administrative busyness: "I am wonderfully well—having no pain of back, or limb, or head. I am careful of my living and exercise; but during the last three years I have worked fifteen hours each day. I have every possible facility of books, retirement and an amanuensis and am doing what I would have to do under less favourable circumstances on my return to Canada."[23] The British Museum he found "a capital place for perfect quiet, for pens and ink, & facilities to get almost any book you want."[24]

Ryerson's *Loyalists* was printed in 1880 by Wm. Briggs, the Methodist printer in Toronto, and not by the august firm of Longmans in London, as he had hoped. The validity of its text depended entirely on the reader's acceptance of the book's basic thesis, towards which its every word argued: that the existence of America as a nation, all of American history and particularly the history of the "Loyalists" are based on a wilful flouting of the laws of God *and* man. A "historical argument" he called it: argument, indeed, it is—total vindication of the "Loyalists" and the British, total damnation to the "rebel Americans" and, even more strongly, to historians like Bancroft who recorded the myths by which Americans lived.

Ryerson looked on the American past with all the prejudices and all the heat generated through decades of Loyalist pride, Methodist defensiveness and a more recently added element of post-Confederation, euphoric "Canadianism." He writes with blinders more firmly adjusted against a wide angle of vision than the American historians whom he impeaches for exaggeration and distortion. Yet, after all this is said, *The Loyalists of America and Their Times* has today its attractions. Its volumes are compendiums of documentation from American and British sources; they are source-books for the Memoirs that, for twenty years, he had collected at first hand from the descendants of the Loyalists themselves. Some of these, Amelia Harris' Memoirs, for example, are classics in our literature.

Ryerson's kind of historian stood at the furthest remove from any notion of dispassionate recording—or of mealy-mouthed defending. He fought a blow-by-blow battle with his literary adversaries as he had bludgeoned John Strachan in the pages of the *Guardian*. And there is, it must be admitted, a pleasant perversity of enjoyment to be had from his blunt readiness to attack the great totem-names of the American past: "It is not easy to squeeze as much extravagance and nonsense in the same space as in the above quoted words of Increase Mather."[25]

Ryerson hoped that his *Loyalists* would be the crowning work of his career, vindicating his past and Canada's, and setting his name within the ranks of the world's scholars. This it did not do: the public were impressed, but the historians whose respect he craved, John Charles Dent, for instance, rejected the work: "No man can be expected to do everything well, and the fact is that Dr. Ryerson did not possess the faculty of writing history. His volumes are laid out with singular want of skill, and the filling-in violates all laws of historical perspective."[26] Even so, there is today a quality commanding wonder in the very toughness of the spirit that drove the pen to write the words; every line of the *Loyalists* beats with Ryerson's unflagging energy and strength of will, engaged in this action, as in all his others, in the affirming of life as he saw it to be lived.

When Egerton Ryerson died in 1882, the men and women he had preached to in the twenties were already dead, or they were aged and in the care of their children and grandchildren in the angular farmhouses that had replaced their log-cabins. To them, and to the generations that had come after them there had indeed been progress, from raw Upper Canada, through the transitions of Canada West, to Ontario—to a reasonably "sunny part of America." And they held, as a cornerstone belief, as solidly there as God himself, a conviction that their Common School System was a very superior one. Why not? They could see its results in progress, from a time when there had been nothing, to a present and a future that were full of hope for their children, and education the gateway to "getting ahead"—towards freedom from a sole dependence on the tyrannical land.

The "public schools" taught literacy; then the High Schools, and their élite the Collegiate Institutes "took in raw material and turned out teachers, more teachers than anything:"

The teachers taught, chiefly in rural districts where they could save money, and with the money they changed themselves into doctors, Fellows of the University, mining engineers. The Collegiate Institute was a potential melting pot: you went in as your simple opportunities had made you; how you shaped coming out depended upon what was hidden in the core of you. You could not in any case be the same as your father before you. . . .[27]

There had not been, nor was there ever to be, one warm encircling dream to successfully join all of Ontario's people. The sharp edges and jagged outlines remained, marking separations of religion, of opportunity and of desire. But the most basic joining of the people ever to be attempted, and within its framework the most successful, was the school system which Egerton Ryerson planned and set in motion.

And though the land was never to be unified to the sight by the grey stone church towers of John Strachan's dream, it did take on a visual unity — through the brick-box school-houses with their squat, "stripped-down-Gothic" belltowers, built in scores of School Sections to Ryerson's plan and approval. For nearly a century they both housed and symbolized the opportunities of a system that matched them to perfection — in their squared-off limits, the confident assertion of the strength of their presence — and in their stolid, but undeniable, dignity.

BIBLIOGRAPHY

A. EGERTON RYERSON. SELECTED WORKS.

The Affairs of the Canadas, in a Series of Letters, by a Canadian. London: J. King, 1837.

Canadian Methodism, Its Epochs and Characterstics. Toronto: W. Briggs, 1882.

Elements of Political Economy, or How Individuals and a Country Become Rich. Toronto: Copp Clark, 1877.

First Lessons in Agriculture for Canadian Farmers and Their Families. Toronto: 1869.

First Lessons in Christian Morals, for Canadian Families and Schools. Toronto: Copp Clark, 1871.

The Grammar School System of Ontario. [Clinton], 1868.

Inaugural Address on the Nature and Advantages of an English and Liberal Education. [Victorial Inaugural, 1842] Toronto: The Guardian Office, 1842.

Letters from the Reverend Egerton Ryerson to the Hon. and Reverend Doctor Strachan. Kingston: The Herald Office, 1828.

The Loyalists of America and Their Times. 2 Vols. Toronto: Wm. Briggs, 1880.

My Dearest Sophie. Ed. by C. B. Sissons. Toronto: Ryerson, 1955.

The School-Book Question. Montreal: John Lovell, 1866.

Sir Charles Metcalfe Defended Against the Attacks of the Late Counsellors. Toronto: 1844.

Special Report on the Systems and State of Popular Education on the Continent of Europe, in the British Isles, and the United States of America. Toronto: Leader Press, 1868.

The Story of My Life. Toronto: Wm. Briggs, 1883.

B. EGERTON RYERSON. BIOGRAPHY AND CRITICISM.

Burwash, Nathanael. *Egerton Ryerson*, in *Makers of Canada*. Toronto: Morang, 1906.

French, Goldwyn. *Parsons and Politics*. Toronto: Ryerson, 1962.

Harris, Robin Sutton. "Egerton Ryerson," in *Our Living Tradition*, ed. Robert MacDougall, 2nd and 3rd series.

Harris, Robin Sutton. *Quiet Evolution, A Study of the Educational System of Ontario*. Toronto: U. of T. Press, [1967].

Hodgins, J. G. *Ryerson Memorial Volume*. Toronto Warwick, 1889.

Putman, J. H. *Egerton Ryerson and Education in Upper Canada*. Toronto: Wm. Briggs, 1912.

Ryerson, George Sterling. *Looking Backward*. Toronto: Ryerson, 1924.

Sissons, Charles Bruce. *Egerton Ryerson, His Life and Letters*. 2 Vols. Toronto: Clarke Irwin, 1937-1947.

C. BACKGROUND MATERIAL. BIOGRAPHICAL AND CRITICAL.

Armstrong, F. H. "Toronto in 1834," in *The Canadian Geographer,* Vol. 10, No. 3, 1966.

Bethune, A. N. *John Strachan.* Toronto: Henry Rowsell, 1870.

Body, Alfred H. *John Wesley and Education.* London: Epworth Press, 1936.

Bosworth, Newton (Rev.). *The Aspect and Influence of Christianity upon the Commercial Character.* Montreal: William Greig, 1837.

Burwash, Nathanael. *The History of Victoria College.* Toronto: Victoria College. Toronto: Victoria College Press, 1927.

Carroll, John Beulah. *Past and Present.* Toronto. Alfred Dredge, 1800.

Carroll, John Beulah. *Case and His Cotemporaries.* Toronto: Samuel Rose, 1867.

Craig, G. M. *Upper Canada, The Formative Years 1784-1841.* Toronto: McClelland & Stewart, 1963.

Davies, Rupert E. *Methodism.* Pelican, 1963.

Dent, John Charles. *The Last Forty Years: Canada Since the Union of 1841.* Toronto: George Virtue, 1881.

Doughty, Sir Arthur, ed. *The Elgin-Grey Papers, 1846-1852.* Ottawa: King's Printer, 1937.

Duncan, Sara Jeannette. *The Imperialist.* Toronto: McClelland & Stewart (New Canadian Library).

Ermatinger, C. O. *The Talbot Regime.* St. Thomas: The Municipal World, 1904.

Ermatinger, E. *Life of Colonel Talbot, and the Talbot Settlement.* St. Thomas: McLachlin, 1859.

Fidler, Isaac. *Observations on Professions, Literature, Manners and Emigration in the United States and Canada Made During a Residence There in 1832.* London: Whittaker, 1833.

Firth, Edith. *The Town of York, 1795-1815 and 1815-1834,* 2 Vols. Toronto: University of Toronto Press, 1962, 1966.

Gill, Frederick C. *The Romantic Movement and Methodism.* London: Epworth Press, 1937.

Gowans, Alan. *Building Canada.* Toronto: Oxford, 1967.

Gowans, Alan. *Images of American Living.* Philadephia: Lippincott, 1964.

Harris, Robin Sutton. "The Beginnings of the Hydrographic Survey of the Great Lakes and the St. Lawrence River," in *Historic Kingston.* No. 14, Kingston Historical Society, 1965.

Harris, Robin Sutton. *Quiet Evolution. A Study of the Educational System of Ontario.* Toronto: University of Toronto Press [1967].

Haw, William (Rev.). *Fifteen Years in Canada.* Edinburgh: Ziegler, 1850.

Head, Sir George. *Forest Scenes and Incidents in the Wilds of North America.* London: John Murray, 1838.

Hilts, Joseph. *Among the Forest Trees.* Toronto: Wm. Briggs, 1888.

Hodgins, John George, ed. *Documentary History of Education in Upper Canada 1791-1876*. 28 Vols. Toronto: Warwick and Rutter, 1894-1910.

Hodgins, John George. *The Establishment of Schools and Colleges in Ontario, 1792-1910*. Toronto: Cameron, 1910.

Jackson, Thomas. *The Centenary of Wesleyan Methodism*. London: John Masow, 1839.

Jameson, Anna Brownell. *Winter Studies and Summer Rambles in Canada*. 3 Vols. in one. New York, [1839?]

(The) *Journal of Education for Ontario* [monthly] 30 Vols. Toronto: J. H. Lawrence, 1848-[77].

Lizars, Kathleen and Robina. *In the Days of the Canada Company*. Toronto: Wm. Briggs, 1896.

MacVey, W. P. *The Genius of Methodism*, Cincinnati: Jennings and Pye, 1903.

Mannoni, O. *Prospero and Caliban: A study of the Psychology of Colonization*. London: Methuen, 1956.

Miller, Perry and Thomas H. Johnson. *The Puritans*, 2 Vols. Harper Torchbooks, 1963.

Moodie, Susanna. *Roughing It in the Bush*. Toronto: McClelland & Stewart, 1962 (New Canadian Library).

Nottingham, Elizabeth K. *Methodism and the Frontier*. New York: Columbia, 1941.

Owen, E. A. *Pioneer Sketches of Long Point Settlement*. Toronto: Wm. Briggs, 1898.

Phillips, C. B. *History of Education in Canada*. Toronto: Gage, 1957.

Playter, George F. *The History of Methodism in Canada*. Toronto: Anson Green, 1862.

Pritchard, F. C. *Methodist Secondary Education*. London: Epworth Press, 1949.

Sweet, W. W. *Methodism in American History*, rev. ed. Nashville, Tenn.: Abingdon Press, 1953.

Taylor, Fennings. "Portraits of British Americans," in A. N. Bethune, *John Strachan*. Toronto: Henry Rowsell, 1870.

Traill, Catharine Parr. *The Backwoods of Canada*. Toronto: McClelland & Stewart, 1966 (New Canadian Library).

Traill, Catharine Parr. *The Canadian Settler's Guide*. Toronto: McClelland & Stewart, 1969 (New Canadian Library).

Warkentin, John. "Southern Ontario: A View from the West," in *The Canadian Geographer*, Vol. 10, No. 3, 1966.

Wesley, John. *The Journal of John Wesley*. Ed. by P. L. Parker. Chicago: Moody Press, n.d.

Whebell, C. F. S. *The Cultural Geography of the Norfolk Sand Plain*. University of Western Ontario, Dept. of Geography, Occasional Papers No. 1.

Withrow, W. H. *The King's Messenger*. Toronto: Methodist Book, 1879.

Withrow, W. H. *Neville Trueman: The Pioneer Preacher*. Toronto: Wm. Briggs, 1880.

NOTES

CHAPTER 1

1. John Beulah Carroll, *Past and Present* (Toronto: Dredge, 1860), p. 293.
2. Egerton Ryerson, *The Story of My Life* (Toronto: Briggs, 1883), pp. 39-43.
3. *Ibid.*, p. 45.
4. *Ibid.*, p. 41.
5. Carroll, *op. cit.*, p. 293.
6. This is one of two portraits of Ryerson painted by Andrew Gush, one in his early thirties and one in middle age.
7. For the history of the Loyalists in Upper Canada, see particularly G. M. Craig, *Upper Canada. The Formative Years, 1784-1841* (Toronto: McClelland & Stewart, 1963), chaps. 1, 3, 9.
8. George Sterling Ryerson, *Looking Backward* (Toronto: Ryerson, 1924), chap. 1.
9. The information in this and the following pages has been taken from Egerton Ryerson's *The Loyalists of America and Their Times*, Vol. II (Toronto: Briggs, 1880), particularly from the recollections of two of Samuel Ryerse's children, George Ryerse and his sister, Mrs. Amelia Harris.
10. Ryerson, *The Loyalists of America and Their Times*, Vol. II, pp. 186-187; from an unidentified pamphlet published in 1784.
11. *Ibid.*, II, p. 187.
12. *Ibid.*, II, p. 187.
13. See G. M. Craig, *op. cit.*, p. 12, for a precise account of the developments and changes in the land-granting policies to Loyalists.
14. Ryerson, *The Loyalists of America and Their Times*, Vol. II, pp. 231-232.
15. cf. Alan Gowans, *Images of American Living* (Philadelphia: Lippincott, 1964); *Building Canada* (Toronto: Oxford, 1967).
16. C. F. S. Whebell, *The Cultural Geography of the Norfolk Sand Plain*, University of Western Ontario, Dept. of Geography, Occasional Papers No. 1, and John Warkentin, "Southern Ontario: A View from the West", *The Canadian Geographer*, Vol. 10, No. 3, 1966, pp. 157-171.
17. Ryerson, *The Story of My Life*, p. 30.
18. E. Ermatinger, *Life of Colonel Talbot and the Talbot Settlement* (St. Thomas, McLachlin, 1859). C. O. Ermatinger, *The Talbot Regime* (St. Thomas, The Municipal World, 1904). Robin S. Harris, "The Beginnings of the Hydrographic Survey of the Great Lakes and the St. Lawrence River", *Historic Kingston*, Kingston Historical Society, No. 14, January, 1966. The biographical information about John and Amelia Harris contained in this article corrects Ermatinger's colourful, but inaccurate account. Eldon House still stands in London, now a museum and a graceful landmark from the past.

19. The character of Amelia Harris which takes form in Ryerson's *My Dearest Sophie* (Toronto: Ryerson, 1955), is one of the pleasures of that collection of letters.

20. cf. Amelia Harris' Memoir in Ryerson's *The Loyalists of America and Their Times* and also E. A. Owen, *Pioneer Sketches of Long Point Settlement* (Toronto: Briggs, 1898).

21. This and the following quotations are taken from Amelia Harris' Memoir, *The Loyalists of America and Their Times*, Vol. II, pp. 232-254.

CHAPTER 2

1. John Wesley, *The Journal of John Wesley*, ed. by P. L. Parker, (Chicago: Moody Press, n.d.), pp. 104-107.

2. Rupert E. Davies, *Methodism* (Pelican, 1963), chaps. 6, 7, 8; W. W. Sweet, *Methodism in American History*, Rev. ed. (Nashville, Tenn.: Abingdon, 1953), chaps. 1-3; Goldwyn French, *Parsons and Politics* (Toronto: Ryerson, 1962), chap. 1, and Elizabeth K. Nottingham, *Methodism and the Frontier* (New York: Columbia, 1941).

3. R. E. Davies, *op. cit.*, pp. 159-160, 163.

4. Ryerson, *Canadian Methodism, Its Epochs and Characteristics* (Toronto: Briggs, 1882), p. 75.

5. Thomas Jackson, *The Centenary of Wesleyan Methodism* (London: John Masow, 1839).

6. Ryerson, *Canadian Methodism*, p. 78.

7. W. P. MacVey, *The Genius of Methodism* (Cincinnati: Jennings and Pye, 1903), p. 56.

8. George F. Playter, *The History of Methodism in Canada* (Toronto: Anson Green, 1862). Goldwyn French, *Parsons and Politics* (Toronto: Ryerson, 1962). For the complicated story of the triumphs and struggles of Methodism in Canada, see Playter for the discursive, anecdotal nineteenth-century version and French for a contemporary historian's documented, detailed, thoroughly expert interpretation, I do not go into the political struggles of Methodism, either its complicated internal strains and schisms or its tensions with government. French has treated both of these areas definitively.

9. Playter, *op. cit.*, I, p. 375.

10. John Beulah Carroll, *Past and Present* (Toronto: Dredge, 1800), p. 112.

11. *Ibid.*, pp. 61-62.

12. John Beulah Carroll, *Case and His Cotemporaries* (Toronto: Samuel Rose, 1867), I, p. 113.

13. *Ibid.*, p. 257.

14. Playter, *op. cit.*, I, p. 260.

15. Carroll, *op. cit.*, I, p. 257.

16. Playter, *op. cit.,* I, p. 55.

17. *Ibid.*, pp. 60-61.

18. *Ibid.*, pp. 61-62.

19. *Ibid.*, p. 84.

20. George Eliot, *Adam Bede* (New York: Pocket Books, 1956), p. 91.

21. Ryerson, *The Story of My Life*, p. 60.

22. *Ibid.*, p. 536.

23. Ryerson, *The Story of My Life*, p. 26.

24. *Ibid.*, p. 26.

25. *Ibid.*, p. 27.

26. *Ibid.*, p. 27.

27. *Ibid.,* p. 27.

28. *Ibid.*, p. 28.

29. *Ibid.*, p. 28.

30. *Ibid.*, p. 29.

CHAPTER 3

1. Ryerson, *The Story of My Life*, p. 44.

2. Playter, *op. cit.*, I, p. 373.

3. Sir George Head, *Forest Scenes and Incidents in the Wilds of North America* (London: John Murray, 1838).

4. Ryerson, *The Story of My Life*, p. 40.

5. Rev. Wm. Haw, *Fifteen Years in Canada* (Edinburgh: Ziegler, 1850), p. 41.

6. *Ibid.*, p. 41.

7. W. H. Withrow, *The King's Messenger* (Toronto: Briggs, 1882), pp. 112-117.

8. Isaac Fidler, *Observations on Professions, Literature, Manners, and Emigration in the United States and Canada Made During a Residence There in 1832* (London: Whittaker, 1833), pp. 284, 313.

9. Edith Firth, *The Town of York*, 1815-1834 (Toronto: University of Toronto Press, 1966), Feb. 27, 1819. cf. also F. H. Armstrong, "Toronto in 1834", *The Canadian Geographer*, Vol. 10, No. 3, 1966, pp. 157-171.

10. Head, *Forest Scenes and Incidents*, pp. 188-189.

11. Henry Schoolcraft, *Personal Memoirs* (Philadelphia: 1851), p. 567.

12. Joseph Hilts, *Among the Forest Trees* (Toronto: Briggs, 1888), p. 12.

13. Isabella Valancy Crawford, "Malcolm's Katie" part II. See also James Reaney's essay on Isabella Valancy Crawford in *Our Living Tradition*, ed. by R. L. MacDougall, 2nd and 3rd series.

14. Anna Jameson, *Winter Studies and Summer Rambles* (New York: [1839?]), I, p. 72.

15. Jameson, *op. cit.*, p. 11.

16. Susanna Moodie, *Roughing It in the Bush* (Toronto: McClelland & Stewart, 1962), p. 77.

17. Ibid., p. 85.

18. Jameson, *op. cit.*, II, p. 21.

19. Moodie, *op. cit.*, p. 25.

20. Jameson, *op. cit.*, II, pp. 329-330.

21. Jameson, *op. cit.*, I, p. 29.

22. Jameson, *op. cit.*, I, p. 306.

23. O. Mannoni, *Prospero and Caliban: A Study of the Psychology of Colonization* (London: Methuen, 1956).

24. Fidler, *op. cit.*, p. 319.

25. Carroll, *op. cit.*, p. 61.

26. Playter, *op. cit.*, p. 278.

27. *Ibid.*, pp. 339, 340.

28. Carroll, *op. cit.*, pp. 63-64.

29. cf. Faulkner, *The Sound and the Fury;* Melville, *Moby Dick,* Father Mapple's Sermon; Playter, Carroll, Withrow, Accounts of Camp Meetings; also, less favourable, Moodie, Jameson, Sherriff.

30. Withrow, *op. cit.*, 174-175.

31. Withrow, *Neville Trueman, The Pioneer Preacher* (Toronto: Briggs, 1880), p. 186. Cf. strong link and direct line to Southern spirituals.

32. Fidler, *op. cit.*, pp. 320-321.

33. Carroll, *op. cit.*, p. 65.

CHAPTER 4

1. J. George Hodgins, *The Establishment of Schools and Colleges in Ontario, 1792-1910* (Toronto: Cameron, 1910), V. 1, p. 2.

2. Ryerson, *The Story of My Life,* p. 52.

3. *Ibid.*, p. 34.

4. *Ibid.*, p. 52.

5. *Ibid.*, p. 47.

6. C. B. Sissons, *Egerton Ryerson,* 2 vols. (Toronto: Clarke, Irwin, 1937, 1947), I, p. 20.

7. Fennings Taylor, "Portraits of British Americans," in A. N. Bethune, *Memoir of the Right Rev. John Strachan* (Toronto: Henry Rowsell, 1870), p. 348.

8. Bethune, *op. cit.*, p. 318.

9. Bethune, *op. cit.*, p. 318.

10. *Ibid.*, p. 137.

11. *Ibid.*, p. 137.

12. Fennings Taylor, in Bethune, *op. cit.*, p. 349.

13. Ryerson, *The Story of My Life*, p. 49.

14. *Ibid.*, p. 51.

15. *Ibid.*, p. 50.

16. Ryerson, *Canadian Methodism*, p. 152.

17. Ryerson, *The Story of My Life*, pp. 58, 59.

18. *Ibid.*, p. 59.

19. *Ibid.*, p. 63.

20. *Ibid.*, p. 67.

21. *Ibid.*, p. 69.

22. *Ibid.,* p. 85.

23. Sissons, *Ryerson*, I, p. 70. J.R. to E.R., Jan. 28, 1828.

CHAPTER 5

1. Ryerson, *The Story of My Life*, p. 93.

2. *Ibid.*, p. 99.

3. *Ibid.*, p. 99.

4. *Ibid.*, p. 101.

5. *Ibid.*, p. 113.

6. Cf. Goldwyn French for a detailed and definitive analysis.

7. Sissons, *Ryerson,* I, p. 163. G.R. to E.R., Apr. 6, 1832.

8. *Ibid.*, I, p. 165.

9. *Ibid.*, I, p. 165.

10. Ryerson, *The Story of My Life*, p. 116, April 16, 1833.

11. Sissons, *Ryerson,* I, p. 183, E.R. to *Christian Guardian,* July 13, 1833.

12. *Ibid.*, p. 181, E.R. to Jas. Armstrong, June 24, 1833.

13. Cf. R. W. Emerson's *English Traits*, close in time and shrewd in analysis but by comparison quite unengaged.

14. Ryerson, *The Story of My Life*, p. 122. *Christian Guardian*, Oct. 30, 1833.

15. Sissons, *Ryerson,* I, pp. 195-196.

16. *Ibid.*, pp. 196-197.

17. *Ibid.*, I, pp. 206, 208, W.R. to E.R., November, 1833.

18. *Ibid.*, I, p. 189, J.R. to E.R., Nov. 7, 1833.

19. *Ibid.*, I, p. 223, J.R. to E.R., Jan. 8, 1834.

20. *Ibid.,* I, p. 221, E.R. to David Wright, Dec. 6, 1833.

21. *Ibid.*, I, p. 220, Jas. Evans to E.R., Dec. 3, 1833.

CHAPTER 6

1. Ryerson, *The Story of My Life*, p. 297, E.R. to John Kent, Dec. 26, 1841.
2. *Ibid.*, p. 284, E.R. in *Christian Guardian*, Oct. 7, 1840.
3. *Ibid.*, p. 244, M. Richey to E.R., July 1, 1839.
4. *Ibid.*, p. 151, E.R. to S. S. Junkin, Sept. 4, 1835
5. *Ibid.*, p. 153, William Lord to E.R., May 31, 1836.
6. *Ibid.*, p. 169, July 21, 1836.
7. *Ibid.*, pp. 175-176, Anson Green to E.R., Nov. 16, 1837.
8. *Ibid.*, p. 177, W.R. to E.R., Dec. 5, 1837.
9. *Ibid.*
10. *Ibid.*, pp. 177-178, W.R. to E.R., Dec. 8, 1837.
11. *Ibid.*, pp. 183-184, J.R. to E.R., April 12, 1838.
12. *Ibid.*, p. 184, W.R. to E.R., April 22, 1838.
13. *Ibid.*, p. 200, J.R. to E.R.
14. *Ibid.*, p. 202, *Christian Guardian*, Aug. 15, 1838.
15. *Ibid.*, pp. 201-202, *Christian Guardian*, July 11, 1838.

CHAPTER 7

1. Ryerson, *The Story of My Life*, p. 261.
2. *Ibid.*, p. 262.
3. *Ibid.*, p. 262.
4. *Ibid.*, p. 262.
5. Perry Miller and Thomas H. Johnson, *The Puritans*, 2 vol. (New York: Harper Torchbooks, 1963), I, p. 60.
6. Sissons, *Ryerson*, II, p. 7, *Christian Guardian*, Feb. 23, 1842.
7. Ryerson, *The Story of My Life*, p. 269, May 1840.
8. *Ibid.*, p. 270, May 25, 1840.
9. *Ibid.*
10. *Ibid.*, p. 276.
11. *Ibid.*, p. 277.
12. Sissons, *Ryerson*, I, p. 577, E. R. to Nathan Bangs, May 10, 1841.
13. *Ibid.*, p. 580, W. S. Conger to E. R., Sept. 3, 1841.
14. Ryerson, *The Story of My Life*, p. 342, E. R. to T. W. C. Murdoch, Jan. 14, 1842.
15. Sissons, *Ryerson*, II, p. 18, *Christian Guardian*, Nov. 3, 1841.
16. *Ibid.*, II, pp. 16-26.
17. *Ibid.*, II, pp. 23-24, Inaugural Address.
18. J. G. Hodgins, *Ryerson Memorial Volume* (Toronto; Warwick, 1889), p. 122.

19. Ryerson, *The Story of My Life*, p. 345. The part which Robert Jameson played in the affairs of Upper Canada from 1833 onward has never been charted by a historian. It was in many instances negative in effect, as here. He did, however, hold high offices and functioned in them; though his presence is always glossed over, or forgotten, it has its interest in the most crucial years of Upper Canada's development.

20. *Ibid*, p. 346, J. R. to E. R., March 6, 1844.

CHAPTER 8

1. Lord Durham's *Report*. Cf. also Putman, *op. cit.*, p. 96.

2. J. G. Hodgins, *Ryerson Memorial Volume*, pp. 109-111.

3. J. G. Hodgins, *Documentary History of Education in Upper Canada* (Toronto: Warwick & Rutter, 1894-1910), vol. 5, pp. 271-286.

4. *Ibid.*, 5, p. 274.

5. *Ibid.*, 5, p. 272.

6. J. H. Putman, *Egerton Ryerson and Education in Upper Canada* (Toronto: Briggs, 1912), p. 94.

7. Hodgins, *op. cit.*, vol. 5, p. 277.

8. *Ibid.*, 5, p. 277.

9. Ryerson, *The Story of My Life*, p. 357.

10. J. G. Hodgins, *op. cit.*, vol. 5, p. 237.

11. Ryerson, *The Story of My Life*, p. 362.

12. *Ibid.*, p. 357.

13. *Ibid.*, p. 362.

14. Hodgins, *op. cit.*, vol. 5, 240.

15. *Ibid.*, 5, p. 240.

16. Ryerson, *The Story of My Life*, p. 357.

17. J. H. Putnam, *op. cit.*, p. 111.

18. Hodgins, *op. cit.*, vol. 6, p. 147.

19. *Ibid.*, vol. 6, p. 142.

20. *Ibid.*, vol. 6, p. 211.

21. *Ibid.*, vol. 6, pp. 142-195.

22. Putman, *op. cit.*, p. 136.

23. Act 9th Victoria, 1846, Hodgins, *op. cit.*, vol. 7; Putnam, *op. cit.*, pp. 123-140.

24. Putman, *op. cit., Ibid.*, p. 124.

25. Hodgins, *op. cit.*, vol. 6, p. 59.

26. *Ibid.*, vol. 6, pp. 59-69.

27. *Ibid.*, vol. 6, p. 199.

28. Putman, *op. cit.*, p. 137.

29. Ryerson, *The Story of My Life,* p. 424.
30. Hodgins, *op. cit.,* vol. 7, p. 115.
31. *Ibid.,* vol. 7, p. 142.
32. *Ibid.,* vol. 7, p. 142.
33. *Ibid.,* vol. 7, p. 147.
34. *Ibid.,* vol. 7, p. 147.
35. *Ibid.,* vol. 7, pp. 137-139.
36. *Ibid.,* vol. 7, pp. 137-149.

CHAPTER 9

1. Ryerson, Egerton, *My Dearest Sophie,* ed. by C. B. Sissons (Toronto: Ryerson, 1955), p. 116.
2. *Ibid,* p. 155.
3. Putman, *op. cit.,* p. 137.
4. *Ibid.,* p. 149. Among the Bill's most important features was the setting aside of £3,000 a year for School Libraries, £25 a year for a Teachers' Institute for each district and a sum for the planning and improving of school architecture, p. 153. These were particularly far-sighted provisions.
5. The *Globe,* January 30, 1851.
6. *Ibid.,* July 16, 1850.
7. Sir Arthur Doughty, ed., *The Elgin-Grey Papers,* 1846-1852 (Ottawa: King's Printer), p. 724.
8. *Ibid.,* p. 736.
9. Ryerson, *The Story of My Life,* p. 516.
10. *Ibid,* p. 456, E.R. to J.G.H., May 2, 1851.
11. Sissons, *Ryerson,* II, pp. 12-13, E.R. to J.G.H., March 12, 1853.
12. Hodgins, *Ibid.,* vol. 7, 1848, p. 178. For detailed discussion of the Separate School Question, see Putman, Ch. VIII, pp. 173-203. The most recent survey of the development of the entire system and of Ryerson's leadership, is to be found in Robin S. Harris, *Quiet Evolution, A Study of the Educational System of Ontario* (Toronto: U. of T. Press, 1967).
13. *Ibid.,* vol. 18, 1866, pp. 304-316.
14. *Ibid.,* vol. 22, 1852, p. 40.
15. Ryerson, *The Story of My Life,* p. 490.
16. Tri-weekly *Globe,* July 11, 1856.
17. Ryerson, *My Dearest Sophie,* July 15, 1864, p. 55.
18. Cf. the entire series of letters in *My Dearest Sophie,* remarkable enough as a portrait of nineteenth-century Upper Canadian life, but especially notable for the warmth, frankness and strength of father-daughter confidence and love.
19. Ryerson, *The Story of My Life,* pp. 516-517.

20. See Sissons, *Ryerson*, II, 347-348, and Hodgins, *Documentary History of Education in Upper Canada*, 13, 1848, p. 209.

21. W. A. Langton, ed., *Early Days in Upper Canada*, (Toronto: Macmillan, 1926), 225 ff.

22. Sissons, *Ryerson*, II, p. 393.

23. Sissons, *Ryerson*, II, p. 366, John Borland to E.R., Feb. 11, 1858.

24. *Ibid.*

25. Ryerson was abundantly honoured by the Methodists in his later years. In 1874 he was elected first President of the General Conference of the three largest groups of Methodists in Canada, then uniting. He was their emissary and their senior statesman until his death. In John Wesley's Chapel, City Road, London, there is a handsome window installed in his memory and in honour of his work for the church.

CHAPTER 10

1. Sissons, *Ryerson*, II, p. 585.

2. *Ibid.*, p. 462, E.R. to the Hon. Sidney Smith, Sept. 5, 1861.

3. Hodgins, *op. cit.*, vol. 16, p. 81.

4. C. B. Phillips, *History of Education in Canada* (Toronto: Gage, 1957). Cf. National Gallery Portrait by Robert Harris, "The School Trustees".

5. Sissons, *Ryerson*, II, pp. 410-411, E.R. to J.G.H., Apr. 27, 1860 and E.R. to Mary R., Apr. 25, 1860.

6. *Ibid.*, II, Chapter XII.

7. Ryerson, *The Story of My Life*, p. 536.

8. *Ibid.*, p. 535.

9. *Ibid.*, p. 537.

10. Ryerson, *My Dearest Sophie*, p. 65.

11. Ryerson, *The Story of My Life*, p. 536 .

12. *Ibid.*, p. 536. This house was torn down about 1965. Now, as a tobacco farm, its land is probably more productive than it ever was during Joseph Ryerson's tenure. The long white frame house, with portico and pillars, was built about 1820, with considerable help from Egerton. It was a fine example of American-classical architecture, imported into Canada. An old barn still remains close to the site of the house.

13. Ryerson, *My Dearest Sophie,* p. 75.

14. cf. Alan Gowans, *Building Canada* (Toronto: Oxford, 1967), especially the text on American classical architecture in Canada.

15. Sissons, *Ryerson*, II, p. 518, E.R. to J.G.J., Jan. 17, 1866.

16. Ryerson, *My Dearest Sophie*, pp. 110-111.

17. Ryerson, *The Story of My Life*, pp. 552-553.

18. *Ibid.*, p. 549.

19. Ryerson, *My Dearest Sophie,* p. 12.
20. *Ibid.*
21. *Ibid.*
22. Ryerson, *The Story of My Life,* p. 581.
23. *Ibid.,* p. 581.
24. Ryerson, *My Dearest Sophie,* p. 300.
25. Ryerson, *The Loyalists of America and Their Times,* I, p. 209.
26. John Charles Dent, *The Last Forty Years: Canada Since the Union of 1841* (Toronto: Virtue, 1881), p. 567.
27. Sara Jeannette Duncan, *The Imperialist* (Toronto: McClelland & Stewart, New Canadian Library), p. 76.

Index